From the moment ⌐⌐⌐⌐⌐⌐⌐ ⌐⌐u will take the gospe⌐ ⌐m has been Matt's soul cry. He's bold, audacious, and carries the fire! Matt has never been anything but steadfast and faithful in his home church. He serves, gives, preaches, and leads in a *constant* manner. He comes from a family that leads with consistency. As a pastor for forty-three years in Chicago, people request weekly to minister at our church. My first questions are always: Where do you serve? Who is your pastor? Do you tithe there? And for how long consistently? The answers to these questions let me know how much an evangelist truly has to impart. Matthew serves here and has for his whole life. I have been his pastor the entire time. He doesn't just talk about giving; he gives every week. This, combined with his prayer life and humble spirit, qualifies Matt to impart. So if you're finally ready for fresh fire, read this book! Matt is the real deal. Your soul will be ABLAZE!

— Dan Willis
Senior Pastor of Lighthouse Church of All Nations, Author of *Freedom to Forget*, *Praise Is My Weapon,* and *The Multicultural Church*

Matt Cruz is a dynamic young man whom the Holy Spirit has raised for such a time as this. His anointed message for this generation to challenge status quo is outlined in *God's Invitation to You*. The Holy Spirit will use this book to turn you from churchgoer to a disciple of Jesus. God's invitation stands. It's time to answer the call!

— Vladimir Savchuk,
Pastor of Hungry Generation Church, Author of *Break Free*

I'm incredibly touched to write this endorsement for evangelist Matt Cruz. I believe with all my heart this is going to be a transformational book that will bring people closer to the Lord

Jesus Christ. Matt has been handpicked by God for such a time as this, a young man for today's generation and tomorrow. He pulls back no punches and preaches the true gospel of Jesus Christ.

— Evangelist John Ramirez,
Author of *Out of the Devil's Cauldron*, *Unmasking the Devil*, and *Armed and Dangerous*

I love what Matt Cruz carries in his life and this message! This book will cause you to take ground everywhere you go. Answer this invitation!

— Pastor Chris Estrada
International Speaker and Author, Chris Estrada Ministries

Salvation is Jesus laying down His life for you. Discipleship is you laying down your life for Him. Heaven isn't just about raising up more voices, but more disciples. Matt Cruz is both a voice and a disciple of Jesus. I truly believe this book will give the next generation a greater understanding of what it is to be a true disciple of Jesus!

— Abram Gomez,
Senior Executive Pastor at Cross Church

Matt Cruz has an uncanny ability to write in a way that makes his book accessible to people in every generation. His book *God's Invitation to You* is one of the most well-rounded, solid books I've read in a long time on the subject matter. It's rare to find somebody in this generation who's rooted and grounded in the Word and values the fruit it produces. Matt Cruz is a trailblazer and a pioneer!

— Dr. Luke Holter,
Author of *Filthy Fishermen*

The message of this book may be the most relevant thing that the body of Christ is to experience during our time. The church has experienced various reformations and revivals, but when we come back to the original intent, the model that Jesus (i.e.: God Himself) walked out for us on this earth, is when we have impact into all spheres of society. Discipleship is the most radical transformation in a person's life. This book's goal is to bring every believer of every denomination into a personal walk with the King of Glory, only then will we truly see Jesus' words come alive: "Here on earth as it is in heaven." I especially love this quote: "He is looking for radical devotion, unreasonable commitment, and undivided dedication." These words are as piercing as a sword, truly causing me to examine my heart and life, to make sure I can honestly claim that I am a *disciple* of Jesus Christ. You will be moved in the depths of your being by the words written by Matt Cruz, and in the process, your heart brought to life—a life of true discipleship.

— Andrey Shapoval,
Pastor of Flame of Fire ministry, Author of *Predestined* and *Big God*

Matt Cruz is a gift to the body of Christ. God has called him to be a voice that stirs this generation to new levels of revival. His book will increase your passion to follow Christ and embolden you to want more of the Spirit's power. When you're done reading, you'll be hungry for His presence!

— Greg Locke,
Pastor of Global Bible Vision church, Author of *This Means War*

Matt Cruz's new book challenges and encourages a young generation to go after Jesus with everything they have. This a must-read for every believer in the body of Christ to have a full understanding of who we are as followers of Christ and what our duties are as disciples and ambassadors for the kingdom. This book will be an inspiration and an awakening for a generation to wake up from their slumber and allow the breath of God to bring life to a breathless, lifeless, hopeless, and helpless generation to be the end-time army of harvesters.

— Mauricio Canales,
Evangelist, Shake the Nations Ministries

The Word tells us that many are called, few are chosen. I believe Matt Cruz has been chosen by the Lord. Matt's dedication to the Lord in the secret place is a testimony to why he is such a powerful evangelist for the kingdom. There is a cost to the anointing, and as one of my close friends, I know firsthand that Matt pays the costly price for this anointing. In this book, he gives incredible insight into the life of a true disciple. If you want to learn practical ways to grow in your calling and destiny in the kingdom, or to do the work of an evangelist—then this book is definitely for you!

— Gilad Rosinger,
Founder of Radiant Israel

GOD'S
INVITATION
to You

MATT CRUZ

*God's Invitation to You: From Passive Christian to
Active Christian*
© 2021 by Matt Cruz. All rights reserved.

Cover and interior design by Cathy Sanders, www.csbookdesign.com.

Printed in the United States of America

ISBN: 978-1-7364216-0-4 (Print)

        978-1-7364216-1-1 (E-book)

DEDICATION

I dedicate this book to my parents, Pastors Frank and Lydia Cruz. Thank you for raising me in the way I should go, so now that I am older I will never depart from it. Thank you for sowing Jesus into my life since I was a little boy, guiding me in the right direction and providing wonderful grounding for a godly life.

ACKNOWLEDGEMENTS

I would like to honor my pastor, Dan Willis, for dedicating me to the Lord as a child, ordaining me as an evangelist, and being my spiritual covering. I'm so thankful for your obedience, integrity, and longevity. Thank you for believing in the next generation and making your ceiling our floor.

I also would like to acknowledge Pastor Jermane Cheatham and Desiree Cheatham for mentoring me when I first was filled with the Holy Spirit. Thank you for your guidance, love, and generosity. I truly am grateful for your lives.

To Isaiah Saldivar and Pastor Ben (Nino), thank you so much for taking me under your wings when I transitioned into full time ministry at a young age. Your guidance, humility, generosity, and love for me have played a crucial role in my life. Thank you for taking me in like family and exemplifying what it is means to be integral, uncompromising, and sold out for the gospel. I love you both very much.

Lastly, I want to shout out to one of my best friends, Adam Pilota, who the Lord used to spark a fire in my heart to host prayer meetings together in my basement. During one of those nights, I was baptized in the Holy Spirit and radically encountered the power and presence of God. Those prayer meetings revolutionized the course of my life. I'm grateful for your friendship and genuine heart.

Thank you to all of the other voices in my life who continue to speak words of encouragement, wisdom, and godly counsel. I honor you all!

CONTENTS

WORK & LEISURE

FOREWORD

FOREWORD

Many of us have experienced the feeling of being torn between two opinions or choices. We all know what it's like to be in the middle of two people arguing when both of them want you to pick their side. We are in a time when the world and the church believe you shouldn't have to pick a side. We live in a day of acceptance and tolerance where nothing seems to be clearly right or wrong anymore. The church has opened itself up to a mixed gospel that says you can "Have the world and have the cross."

In this book, Matt Cruz plays the role of Elijah in our generation. While reading this book, this phrase that Elijah uttered in 1 Kings 18:21 kept coming to my mind, "Elijah approached all the people and said, 'How long will you hesitate between two opinions? If the Lord is God, follow Him; but if Baal, follow him.' But the people [of Israel] did not answer him [so much as] a word." Like Elijah, Matt Cruz is calling the church to pick a side!

We no longer have the luxury to live in the middle ground. If you're tired of average, dead, and dry religion, this book will light a fresh fire in your soul. If you're looking for something to challenge the status quo and provoke you to good works, look no further.

Knowing Matt Cruz personally, this is not merely a book he wrote, but a lifestyle I have watched him live. He is a true modern-day Phillip (the only official evangelist mentioned in Scripture). The good news is that Matt Cruz is calling every single believer to the role of the evangelist. In fact, this is what Jesus called all of us to in the great commission. If I could sum this book up in one sentence, it would be straight out of chapter 3, "You are more than just some member at a church or some congregant; you are a soldier in the army of God!"

You will not be able to finish this book with an open mind and stay the same. So what are we waiting for? The harvest is plentiful, but the laborers are few. Let's accept God's invitation, stop making excuses, and start making disciples!

— **Isaiah Saldivar**
Revivalist

INTRODUCTION:
MY TESTIMONY

INTRODUCTION: MY TESTIMONY

My name is Matt Cruz. I am twenty-four years old and was born and raised in Chicago, Illinois. I grew up in the church, but all that time I still lived like the world. I was just a churchgoer, not a disciple of Jesus; I claimed to be saved, but Jesus was never the Lord of my life. I did love God, and I was even plugged into a lot of church programs growing up—but the problem I had was being apathetic and lukewarm. I loved God and claimed to know Him, but I denied Him by my actions. I had enough of God in my life to not enjoy the world—but I also had enough of the world in my life to not enjoy God. While going through the motions for years, I told my parents I will never preach. My mom always told me, "Be careful what you say, because God might just do the opposite and use you to preach."

I worked for a police department at the age of eighteen. I attempted to enlist into the Marine Corps, and then move to Florida to become a cop. I had everything planned out. But then one night in the basement of my home I had a serious encounter with the person of Jesus. That night, I exchanged my ambitions, my goals, and my dreams for the plan of God. He revealed that He had a purpose for my life long before I had a plan for myself. I am a witness that sometimes your plans have to fail so God's purpose can prevail! His plans are far greater than the plans we have for ourselves.

I wanted to be a soldier so badly; that was my passion. I saw my brother graduate from the Marine Corps in San Diego California when I was little boy, and in that moment I fell in love with the marching, the cadence, and militant attitude.

His plans are far greater than the plans we have for ourselves.

But that night when I encountered Jesus in my basement, I enlisted into a different army. I became empowered for God's service. There was a holy fire ignited in my heart to dutifully obey His marching orders—to lift up the name of Jesus Christ and put down my own name. That night, I committed to ministering the gospel with boldness and to do exactly what I had told my parents I would never do—preach! I was commissioned to walk in love and remind people that they are not their own; they belong to God, and to encourage them to take up their cross and follow Him.

That night I committed myself to love Him, obey Him, and serve Him all the days of my life. It was the greatest joy I have ever experienced. It has now been five years, and I have traveled around the world to so many places—and still continue to travel almost every weekend. I have seen God move in ways I never could have imagined! I have seen atheists, Muslims, Hindus, agnostics, and more come to the personal knowledge of who Jesus is. I have seen deaf ears and blind eyes open. I have seen cancer healed. I have seen demons flee. There is power in the name of Jesus! In the last five years I have reached over 200 million people online, and I am blown away by that. Life without Jesus is truly a dead end. He is the One who called me out of darkness into His marvelous light. He is the One who turns bondage into freedom and sin into salvation.

There is no one like Him! When I tasted Jesus, the rest of the world lost its flavor. God didn't create us for *us*; He created us for *Him*! For it is in Him that we live and move and have our being. Your life is not a mistake. If you have never experienced this joy, peace, and love, I advise you to give Him a try. If you repent of your sins, He will be faithful and just to forgive you. I don't care what you have done or how messed up your past is—you are never too lost to be saved, and you are not too dirty for God to cleanse. And you are not too guilty for God to forgive! He will wash you clean and make you white as snow, as if you've never committed those sins; as if that was never the person you were. That is the gospel! While we were lost, He died, He rose from the dead, and He demonstrated that He is God. Then we turn from our sin and trust Him. Those who call on the name of the Lord shall be saved.

Your life is not a mistake. If you have never experienced this joy, peace, and love, I advise you to give Him a try.

I have experienced this for myself, and because of it, I will never turn off the switch of my faith. All it takes is one encounter with the King of Kings! What are you waiting for? People will miss heaven by eighteen inches; because that's the distance from your head to your heart. The light of truth cannot be turned on for you; you can only be shown the switch. Tomorrow is not promised. Now is the day of salvation!

> "What no eye has seen, what no ear has heard, and what no human mind has conceived"—the things God has prepared for those who love him. (1 Corinthians 2:9)

> If you declare with your mouth, "Jesus is Lord, and believe in your heart that God raised him from the dead, you will be saved." (Romans 10:9)

CHAPTER 1: FROM CHURCHGOER TO DISCIPLE

CHAPTER 1: FROM CHURCHGOER TO DISCIPLE

People today freely confess that they are Christians, but few will admit that they are disciples. A Christian is not merely one who claims to believe in Jesus, but also one who is committed to Him and sincerely follows His teachings. God isn't looking for those who claim to be Christians. He isn't looking to see what denomination or religion you claim. He is looking for disciples who will follow Him day in and day out, through the trials of life as well as the victories in life. When Jesus called His disciples to follow Him, they ate, drank, sweat, and slept ministry from that point on until the day they died. Jesus wasn't just a part of their lives; He *was* their life. It should be the same for us. He is the author of life, and following Him requires everything. He is the all in all.

We are all guilty of putting things above Jesus. Whether it is health, wealth, comfort, dreams, hobbies, or interests, we all come to Jesus with expectations of what He will do for us. We all have our passions, but Jesus isn't concerned with our comfort; He came to take over; He wants to sit in the driver's seat of our lives. The gospel is free, but it requires those who follow to lose their life so that Christ may live in them instead.

I grew up in church all my life, but I found myself merely going through the motions of Christianity. I had no prayer life, no devotion life, and no passion. I was only a Christian on Sunday morning, not throughout the week. Many people come to Jesus thinking that it is enough to believe, to stand on the sidelines and root for Him. But He isn't looking for cheerleaders—He is seeking men and women who will follow Him no matter what it costs them. He is looking for radical devotion, unreasonable commitment, and undivided dedication. Jesus isn't looking for churchgoers; He's looking for disciples. He's not even looking for congregants. He's looking for those who will be faithful and committed!

Take a look at the difference between churchgoers and disciples:

- Churchgoers are believers who live like the world. Disciples are believers who live like Jesus.
- Churchgoers are focused on their values, interests, worries, fears, priorities, and lifestyles. Disciples are focused on Jesus.
- Churchgoers go to church. Disciples are the church.
- Churchgoers are involved in the mission of Jesus. Disciples are committed to it.

- Churchgoers cheer from the sidelines. Disciples are in the game.
- Churchgoers hear the word of God. Disciples live it.
- Churchgoers follow the rules. Disciples follow Jesus.
- Churchgoers are all about believing. Disciples are all about being.
- Churchgoers are comfortable. Disciples make sacrifices.
- Churchgoers talk. Disciples make more disciples.

You may be asking, "What is a disciple, Matt?" I'm glad you asked. A disciple is someone who wholeheartedly follows the life and example of Jesus; who makes His mission their mission, His values their values, and His heart their heart. A disciple is someone who desperately seeks to be like Jesus. A disciple is someone so committed to the cause of Christ that they would follow Him through the gates of hell and back. A disciple is someone who finds their identity, purpose, and meaning in Jesus. He is the center of their lives! They are all in—fully committed. Not only is a disciple willing to die for Jesus, but they are dedicated to living every day of their life for Him.

To become a disciple means to become a life-long learner, a student of Jesus Christ. We never stop growing in the grace and knowledge of Jesus. We need to stop acting like we know it all. Disciples understand their need for a savior and the strength only He can give. I never want to be a know-it-it-all, I want to be a learn-it-all. Followers of Jesus will always be learning, and after proper discipleship, they become a maker of disciples. I've learned that the discipleship process begins internally, within the heart. The internal change that takes place in the heart results in the external change of one's behavior, mindset, and lifestyle.

Jesus offers us grace and love without condition, but not without expectation. Many today try to water down the message by saying things like, "You don't have to give up sin. You don't have to change. You don't have to be transformed. You don't have to die to yourself. You just need to believe." But in doing this, not only are they depriving people of the truth, they are denying them access to a real, transforming relationship with almighty God. The devil is not afraid of people going to church, he is afraid of people starting to look like Christ. What are you doing to become more like Him?

Christianity isn't just a system of belief; it is a life transformed by Jesus.

Christianity isn't just a system of belief; it is a life transformed by Jesus. It's a life committed to Him and His Word. We cannot claim to be followers of Jesus and not live in His word. Being in relationship with Him, and not reading His Word is like swimming without water. His Word must become the compass that we rely on for direction.

His call for each of us is different, but the call is an extreme standard: Jesus must be greater than everything else.

Characteristics of a Disciple of Jesus

A Disciple Is Obedient and Devoted to the Word of God

A disciple is one who has committed himself to the gospel. Scripture says, "So the word of God spread. The number of disciples in Jerusalem increased rapidly, and a large number of priests became obedient to the faith" (Acts 6:7; cf. 14:22). When one is obedient to the gospel of Christ, they are a disciple or follower of Christ. Have we sincerely committed ourselves to the gospel? If so, we are disciples of Jesus.

A Disciple Is Submitted to Christ

Are we truly submitted to the teachings of Jesus? Are faithful to Him, even when it requires sacrifice on our part? Do we submit to His Word, even when it means we must reject deeply rooted sins, turn from false religion, die to "self"—to what we want, what we feel, and what we think, so that the will and mind of Jesus will rule in us? If we do, then we manifest true discipleship.

A Disciple Is One Who Genuinely Loves Others

Love is another primary trait of one who is a disciple of Jesus. Jesus says, "A new command I give you: Love one another. As I have loved you, so you must love one another. By this everyone will know that you are my disciples, if you love one another" (John 13:34–35). A disciple of Christ is not one who is selfish and unconcerned; rather, he is one who genuinely loves other believers (and all people)—for in this way, we display to others that we are true disciples of Jesus.

A Disciple Is a Lover of Jesus

Jesus said something that must have shaken His hearers in their hearts. "If anyone comes to me and does not hate father and mother, wife and children, brothers and sisters—yes, even their own life—such a person cannot be my disciple" (Luke 14:26). Jesus said that to become His true disciple, one must be willing to "hate" everyone else! In other words, our love for the Lord Jesus must be so deep and intense, so passionate and all-consuming, that every other "love" seems like "hate" in comparison! Jesus explains further in Matthew 10:37: "Anyone who loves their father or mother more than me is not worthy of me; anyone who loves their son or daughter more than me is not worthy of me." He is the King of love and must become the King of our hearts if we claim to be His true follower.

Jesus said that the greatest command is: "Love the Lord your God with all your heart and with all your soul and with all your mind and with all your strength" (Mark 12:30). Love for Christ is the primary trait of a disciple of Jesus.

A Disciple Is Fruit-Bearing

A Christian who is filled with the Holy Spirit is enabled to produce the fruit of love, joy, peace, patience, kindness, goodness, faithfulness, gentleness, and self-control (Galatians 5:22–23), as well as righteousness and truth (Ephesians 5:9). Jesus said, "This is to my Father's glory, that you bear much fruit, showing yourselves to be my disciple" (John 15:8). We demonstrate our discipleship when we manifest God's fruit in our life.

A Disciple Is One Who Denies Himself

Jesus said plainly, "Whoever wants to be my disciple must deny themselves and take up their cross daily and follow me" (Luke 9:23). We are living in a very self-indulgent age; most people do what they want to do, when they want to do it, and how they want to do it. People don't discipline themselves to say no and change their lives according to what they know to be right. They are addicted to alcohol, tobacco, drugs, food, music, sleep, entertainment, and more. Jesus said that if we wish to follow Him, then as His disciple, we need to say no to ourselves! The spirit of "me" is what is in our way. Jesus shakes us from our self-indulgent apathy by saying that we must "hate" our own life (Luke 14:26) or "hate" our own "life in this world" (John 12:25). This means that we must turn from following the flesh and our self-will and begin to follow Jesus and His will. It's time to stop *satisfying* your flesh and start *crucifying* your flesh. My friend once said, "If we don't crucify our flesh privately, our flesh will crucify us publicly."

Not only must a disciple be willing to deny themselves, but they must also be willing to carry their cross. Jesus declared, "Whoever does not carry their cross and follow me cannot be my disciple" (Luke 14:27). I was studying the cross, and in the first century, it was an instrument of execution. To carry our cross means that we must be willing to lay down our life for Christ and suffer persecution, hardship, and trials to follow the Lord as a disciple. We must "die" to ourselves and sin, and even be willing to die physically if need be. Most people want to follow the most pleasing path to the flesh and have a comfortable and pleasant experience. Romans 8:6 says, "The mind governed by the flesh is death, but the mind governed by the Spirit is life and peace." In other words, if our flesh is driving, we will always end up down a destructive path. Jesus says that we must be willing to die for Him. We must realize that suffering is part of living for Christ (see Acts 14:22; 2 Timothy 3:12).

A Disciple Must Actively Follow Jesus

Jesus said, "Whoever serves me must follow me; and where I am, my servant also will be. My Father will honor the one who serves me" (John 12:26). When Jesus was alive, His disciples followed Him from place to place and heard Him speak to people with their own ears. In our day, we need to allow Him to speak through Scripture's written words (see Hebrews 1:1–2; Colossians 3:16). It is time to allow God's voice to become the loudest one we hear and the one to which we are most sensitive. When we follow the Lord Jesus, we will "live as Jesus did" and keep His words (1 John 2:3–6).

A Disciple Must Forsake All for Christ

The Lord Jesus said plainly, "Those of you who do not give up everything you have cannot be my disciples" (Luke 14:33). This verse speaks of complete and uncompromising surrender of all that one is and has, which was fulfilled when Jesus called Peter and Andrew to be His disciples. He commanded, "Come, follow me . . . and I will send you out to fish for people" (Mark 1:17). Their response: "At once they left their nets and followed him" (Mark 1:18). He also called James and John, who likewise left their occupation and followed Jesus (see Mark 1:20). In a very real sense, we, too, must leave everything behind—our plans, our lifestyle, our independent way of living, and anything in our life that would displease our Lord. Jesus deserves all, and He demands all. He may allow us to use certain possessions, but we will never actually own them as we did before coming to Christ. Jesus will become our "all"—our very life (see Philippians 1:21; Colossians 3:4).

A Disciple Is a Disciple-Maker

A disciple teaches others how to live the Christian life. Jesus told us to be "fishers of men." If you know anything about fishermen, it is not enough for them to go to fishing conferences, buy bait at a tackle shop, or talk about how to fish—without ever fishing. In the same way, we need to be growing in our understanding of Jesus while teaching others to do the same. Jesus instructed his followers, "Therefore go and make disciples of all nations, baptizing them in the name of the Father and of the Son and of the Holy Spirit" (Matthew 28:19 NIV). Jesus doesn't stop there; he continues in verse 20, "And teaching them to obey everything I have commanded you."

CHAPTER 2:
COMFORT-ZONE
CHRISTIANITY

CHAPTER 2: COMFORT-ZONE CHRISTIANITY

Comfort-zone Christianity is more about us than it is about Jesus. We want our churches to be on fire, yet all we do is focus on them being cool. When we make the house of God an entertainment venue, we will find ourselves blending in with secular culture. We don't go to church to see how close we can get to what the world does. There's so much of the world in the church today, and vice versa, that it's hard to tell the difference. We don't go to church to be entertained; we go to church to be equipped! Truth is better than entertainment. I would rather offend someone into heaven than flatter them into hell. If it doesn't challenge us, how will it change us? I am all about being all things to all men so that we will win them, but sugar-coated ear-candy preaching is what keeps believers in their comfort zone. Preaching the message of Christ should challenge us to be more like Jesus—and becoming more like Him always requires discomfort. We don't grow when we're comfortable. I heard a man of God say, "We are called to afflict the comfortable and comfort the afflicted." God calls us to comfort others, but the problem is that we would rather comfort ourselves. We even have comfort foods! Friend, comfort isn't necessarily bad, but our ultimate comfort should not be dependent upon things or circumstances, but rather upon God. He isn't concerned with our comfort as much as He is our obedience.

While being active in ministry, I've come to realize that discomfort has the potential to help us grow closer to God and to depend on Him, and it allows Him to show Himself strong on our behalf. God has a way of testing us, stretching us, and shaping us in uncomfortable ways—ways we would never choose for ourselves. If we look at the word of God, Jesus often led His disciples out of their comfort zone and into uncomfortable—even dangerous—situations.

Discomfort has the potential to help us grow closer to God and to depend on Him, and it allows Him to show Himself strong on our behalf.

In Matthew chapter 14, one-night Jesus sent Peter and the other disciples ahead of Him in a small boat, knowing that a raging storm was on its way. During that frightening storm, Jesus came to them like a ghost, walking on the dark water in the middle of the sea, unmoved by the wind and the waves. To prove He was Jesus, He instructed Peter to get out of the boat and walk on the water toward Him. This was an ultimate out-of-the-comfort-zone moment! Peter's obedience and quick faith allowed him to walk on water, but fear almost drowned him when he took his focus off of Jesus.

Jesus used discomfort to show His miraculous power that night. Jesus and Peter walked on water, and then Jesus rescued Peter and the other disciples by calming the storm, and then He accepted their worship. When we obey God's voice, take steps of faith outside of our comfort zone, and focus on Jesus, miracles can happen. If we recognize Jesus as God, we can trust Him in any situation. Jesus is our Comforter. When He calls us out of our comfort zone, He is not calling us to be comfortable in the situation; He's calling us to be comfortable in Him *in spite of* the situation. He is the One who saved us. Jesus deserves our trust and our worship, regardless of our circumstances. He is the way-maker and mountain-mover!

The Heroes of Faith

Throughout Scripture, God calls ordinary people to do big things—things outside their comfort zone. And what makes them extraordinary, what makes them our Bible heroes, is simply that they obediently stepped out of their comfort zone in faith. They weren't great men and women. They simply did great things for God in obedience.

- Moses was called to leave his job of shepherding sheep to confront Pharaoh and lead an entire nation of people to freedom.
- Joshua was commanded to lead the fearful Israelites into battle and into freedom so they could take hold of their Promised Land.
- Nehemiah was called to leave his comfortable job in a palace and become the leader who would help rebuild the wall around Jerusalem.
- Gideon was called to leave his job threshing wheat and lead a small group of warriors to defeat the very people they had been hiding from.
- Esther was challenged to approach the king, though it was against the law to do so without being invited, in the hope that it would save her people from annihilation.
- Mary was called to become a teenage mother before she had even become a wife. And not just any mother—the mother of the long-awaited Savior.
- Jesus was called to die an excruciating death on a cross so that you and I could be saved.
- The uneducated disciples were called to go out into the world and make disciples of all nations despite harsh persecution.
- Paul was called to preach to the very people he had been persecuting, as well as to those who had been doing the persecuting along with him.[1]

1. Jenn Soehnlin, "Embracing Courage Rather Than Your Comfort Zone," *Embracing Life* (Blog), posted July 27, 2018, accessed December, 28, 2020, https://embracing.life/article/embracing-courage-rather-than-comfort-zone.

CHAPTER 2: COMFORT-ZONE CHRISTIANITY

What I find encouraging is that some of the people in the Bible made excuses, too. They felt inadequate, timid, too young, or too unqualified. But they were obedient anyway.

They had their doubts and their fears, just like us. But they chose to do what God called them to do. Moses, who felt unqualified to speak to Pharaoh because of his speech, would be the one to confidently lead God's people and to tell Joshua to "Be strong and courageous, for you must go with this people into the land . . . The Lord himself goes before you and will be with you; he will never leave you nor forsake you. Do not be afraid; do not be discouraged" (Deuteronomy 31:7–8).

Esther, who was fearful of the fatal consequence of approaching the king without an invitation, courageously tells Mordecai to fast and pray for her and says, "If I perish, I perish" (Esther 4:16).

Mary, who was a little unsure about the logistics of getting pregnant before being married and timid about all the responsibility that would come with raising the Messiah, still said, "I am the Lord's servant . . . May your word to me be fulfilled" (Luke 1:38).

The night before His death, Jesus, in great sorrow, told God, "Father, if you are willing, take this cup from me; yet not my will, but yours be done" (Luke 22:42). Then He obediently went to the cross, putting God's plan ahead of His own fears and desires.

41

Paul, who experienced unimaginable hardships while preaching to and planting churches, said he was "Paul, a servant of Christ Jesus, called to be an apostle and set apart for the gospel of God" (Romans 1:1).

It really is up to us. We have to make a decision to put our faith into action. The bible says faith without works is dead. You can choose to be courageous, or you can choose to be comfortable. You can choose to be obedient or continue to live in fear. There is always an action component to the call of God. Rarely can we stay where we are and do what we've always been doing and fulfill the call of God upon our lives. We've got to *go*!

An Uncomfortable Situation Brings Breakthrough

In June of 2019, some friends and I hosted revival meetings in seven different cities in Texas. On the Saturday of our last weekend in the state, we were ministering in a town named Alice. This small building was packed with hundreds of people seated very close together. I was scheduled to preach that night, and before I was headed to the pulpit, my friend Brandon opened up for me. He started talking about the power of the Holy Spirit and His desire to deliver us. In a moment, half of the congregation started manifesting demonic spirits—so many demons were groaning and yelling through people as the power and fire of almighty God was displayed! We were there for hours praying over people as God delivered them from demonic strongholds. I didn't even preach; God had a different plan. It was a glorious night as many received true breakthrough and freedom.

That next morning, I had to preach near Dallas, which was about a six-hour drive from where we were. We drove through the night and arrived an hour before the service started. Brandon and my cousin Justin were the only ones with me. Everyone else had left early in the morning to go back home for Father's Day weekend. Brandon and Justin were so tired that they told me they were going to head to the hotel and would meet me later.

After I preached two services, the pastor dropped me off at the hotel. When I got to the room, Brandon and Justin began to tell me about the crazy interaction they had with the hotel clerk while I was preaching. As they walked up to the front desk to check in, he greeted them and asked what they were in town for. They replied that they were in town preaching the gospel of Jesus Christ. At that point the hotel clerk immediately started treating them differently. He told my cousin and Brandon to get away from the desk and that he wouldn't check them in.

Confused, Justin and Brandon tried to contact me, but I was on stage preaching. They exited the hotel and tried calling the pastor who booked the room for us. While they were out front, my cousin Justin started thinking about all the wonderful things God had done the night before in Alice. He told Brandon that that the enemy was mad because all those people had gotten delivered. So he reached in his pocket and took out cash to bless the hotel clerk. He went back in the hotel and walked up to the front desk, reached out his hand, and apologized to the hotel clerk if they had said anything wrong.

As he started loving on the man, God pierced the clerk's heart with compassion. The clerk explained that the reason he didn't check them in was because the moment they mentioned the name of Jesus, it reminded him of his wife who had left him for a pastor ten years ago. Brandon and Justin ministered to the man, and that bitterness left his heart. He said he never wanted to treat another minister wrong ever again. Praise God!

Distraction: The Enemy of Focus

Our comfort is either killing our encounter or someone else's. We need to learn how to get comfortable being uncomfortable! In that situation with the hotel clerk, instead of thinking about how hard it was to not act out in their flesh and yell back at the man, they focused on asking the Lord to enlarge their understanding. They got out of the comfort zone and blessed the man!

> But I tell you, love your enemies and pray for those who persecute you. (Matthew 5:44)

That man was going through something, and instead of getting worked up and yelling back at him, Justin moved beyond his boundaries and followed the leading of the Holy Spirit. The devil tried to distract them with the clerk's attitude—but distraction is the enemy of focus. We are constantly tempted to pull away from a consistent focus on Christ. As a result, we often find ourselves being tossed to and fro by the concerns of life. Keeping focus on Jesus means that we are purposefully fading out everything that pulls us away from connecting with Him. It is a disciplined lifestyle of choosing to see every blessing and struggle through the lens of Christ.

You cannot expect God to be the source of your peace if the world is the source of your satisfaction!

How can we stay focused in a world of "busyness"? Isaiah 26:3 says, "You will keep in perfect peace those whose minds are steadfast, because they trust in you." When we focus on Him, He will give us perfect peace. Think about that. Not some peace or a little peace—but *perfect* peace. You cannot expect God to be the source of your peace if the world is the source of your satisfaction!

Evaluate what is distracting you from God. Ask yourself which aspects of your life are pulling you further away from God. Pressures and responsibilities, such as work, school, and relationships, are common distractions. All of those things will keep you in your comfort zone and prevent you from growing in your faith. You cannot grow your faith inside of your comfort zone. Our lack of intimacy with God causes a void that we try to fill with the frailest of substitutes.

The more you focus on yourself, the more distracted you will be from the proper path. The more you know Him and commune with Him, the more the Spirit will make you like Him. The more you are like Him, the better you will understand how much you need God for all of life's difficulties. And that is the only way to know real satisfaction.

You cannot grow your faith inside of your comfort zone.

Later that year, I was back in Texas again with my buddy Brandon. I was preaching two days in a row in south Texas. On my last day preaching, we got some rest and woke up the next day to check out. We were on a tight schedule—I was preaching in another conference an hour away from where we were staying. But before we went there, I needed to get something done at the bank. I searched for the location of the bank in my GPS, and it said it was only four minutes away. As we were pulling up to the ATM, we got stopped by a train. We couldn't waste any more time, so I said we would just wait two minutes for this train to get past, then everything would be okay. But then, out of nowhere, the train stopped, and then it started moving backward! I was so frustrated because I needed to get to the bank, but this train was preventing me from doing so. We ended up turning around and hitting the highway.

Ten minutes later, a Porsche zoomed past us. Then a state trooper pulled close behind our vehicle before pulling us over. I gave her my driver's license, and she said she would be right back. As she was running my license, Brandon looked at me and said, "Matt, we need to pray for this state trooper." I was in my comfort zone, still frustrated about the bank situation, and I just wanted to get to the other conference on time. She came back again, and Brandon started prophesying over her. This state trooper started crying and was touched by the love of God. She let us go, and as we were on the road, it hit me—the train that stopped us was all in God's plan to turn us around so we could run into that state trooper and allow God to reach her heart through our obedience.

Focusing on what the Holy Spirit is doing puts our eyes on the Father's intended outcome for a situation—and that is what provokes us to move without hesitation out of our comfort zone. Focusing on God's heart positions us to fulfill His purposes.

Focusing on Jesus

We need to be able to perceive where the Spirit's anointing is and what God is doing so we can follow Him. Even when a situation is at its worst, we can step back into our spirits and sense what the Holy Spirit desires in that moment. The kingdom of God will not be advanced by our churches being filled with men and women, but by men and women in our churches becoming filled with God. When we allow the Holy Spirit to give us focus, we experience God's power, His intention, His faithfulness, His love, and His greatness.

The kingdom of God will not be advanced by our churches being filled with men and women, but by men and women in our churches becoming filled with God.

Even our own flaws can distract us from keeping our eyes on Jesus. If we think too much about what is wrong with us, we will forget what God can do through us. If we look too much at what we lack, we will forget to be thankful for what we have.

The Bible says to look away from all that distracts us from focusing on Jesus (see Hebrews 12:2). If your faith begins to waver, quickly get your eyes back on Jesus, who is the source of your faith and the reason for your belief. Remember how He endured the cross, despising and ignoring the shame of it, for the joy of winning you to Himself! People complain about stress, but some people would rather complain than change. If we can be honest, some of us only let God in enough to comfort us—and not enough to cause us to change! God wants you to enjoy a life of power and clear direction. That only comes by spending time with Him, reading His Word, talking to Him, and listening for His response. If you are too busy to get alone with Him each day, then you need to set some boundaries in your life. Say no to whatever is keeping you from starting your day with God. Nothing can compare to being with Him! Until we are with Him, we cannot say we know Him.

CHAPTER 3:
SPIRITUAL ZOMBIE

CHAPTER 3: SPIRITUAL ZOMBIE

T hree thousand years ago, God gave the prophet Ezekiel a vision. Ezekiel said, "The hand of the Lord was upon me, and he brought me out by the Spirit of the Lord and set me in the middle of a valley; it was full of bones. He led me back and forth among them, and I saw a great many bones on the floor of the valley, bones that were very dry" (Ezekiel 37:1–2).

Imagine the scene in your mind of thousands of bones spread out across the valley. The bones are in bad shape. They are scattered, disordered, and dry.

The Spiritually Lost

These dry bones represent our world today. Look at the government, politics, and the news. We see much chaos, broken homes, divorce, violence, poverty, and human trafficking. People are scattered, disorganized, and are fighting with one another. People are canceling others because they don't believe or think the way they do. People celebrate what is evil and condemn what is good. People value reason over faith, tolerance over truth, and pleasure over purpose. The world is in bad shape.

Without Christ, people are dead. We are surrounded by a valley of dry bones that need to be resurrected.

Without Christ, people are dead. We are surrounded by a valley of dry bones that need to be resurrected.

The Spiritually Dead

Ezekiel prophesied, just like the Lord commanded. As he was prophesying, there was a noise; a rattling sound, and the bones came together, bone to bone.

But there was still a problem. Ezekiel says, "I looked, and tendons and flesh appeared on them, and skin covered them, but there was no breath in them" (Ezekiel 37:8). In this verse, the scattered bones came together, but the bodies were not breathing.

These bones without breath represent dead churches and powerless Christians. These zombie bodies represent churches that look organized, but are spiritually dead. They represent Christians who carry on with their compromise and complacency instead of allowing God to sit in the driver's seat of their life. There are entire denominations that look great organizationally, but the Holy Spirit is not moving.

These bodies are like zombies; they look alive, but they are really dead. Likewise, many Christians look spiritual, but in reality, they are lifeless. They never do anything with what is on the inside of them. They never go out witnessing; they just sit in church and never accomplish anything. Jesus didn't save you to just come into church and be blessed. He didn't save you so you can hear a nice, cute sermon and feel better. You are more than just some member at a church or some congregant; you are a soldier in the army of God!

You might be reading this and thinking to yourself, "Matt, how can I know if I'm a spiritual zombie?" You might be one if you are spiritually stagnant. Dead bodies stink!

In 2018, I took a tour with my pastor to Israel. While we were there, we visited the Dead Sea, which is the lowest place on earth. The Dead Sea has water coming in but none going out. The water stagnates and begins to stink. If a person sits in church just receiving all the time, but never has an outlet to give to others, they will begin to stagnate.

We have been filled up to be poured out! We are called to be an outlet for the love of Christ to flow through us everywhere we go. When people meet us, they should meet Him.

You might be a spiritual zombie if you are spiritually complacent. Dead bodies do not move. These are people who are living in a comfort zone; they exist at a lower level than God has called them to. They do not use their gifts, talents, or abilities for God. There is an epidemic of complacency that is sweeping into the church. It is being infiltrated by culture, causing believers not to be truly committed to God.

The Spiritually Living

God told Ezekiel to prophesy again. He said, "Prophesy to the breath; prophesy, son of man, and say to it, 'This is what the Sovereign Lord says: Come, breath, from the four winds and breathe into these slain, that they may live'" (Ezekiel 37:9). So Ezekiel prophesied as God commanded, and suddenly breath entered the dead bodies; they came to life and stood to their feet!

> **It's time to stop being shaky about what we believe and start being shaken by what we believe.**

There are many people in the world and in church who have dry bones, who are spiritually dead, who need to hear the Word of the Lord. They need the Lord to awaken them and breathe new life into their bones! God wants to show us the reality of trusting only in Him and allowing Him to awaken what is dead in our lives. It's time to stop being shaky about what we believe and start being shaken by what we believe.

What in the world would God want with dry bones? The spiritually dead? The lukewarm? It just goes to show us that God wants all of us or none of us. I heard a preacher say one time that part-time Christians cannot defeat full time devils. God doesn't want partnership with us—He wants ownership of us! Don't ride the fence. If you do, someone is going to knock you off, and it's going to hurt! Turn your eyes to Jesus, who is the source of our faith and the reason for our belief.

He is the life-giver, and He has come to breathe new life into us. He strongly desires to breathe life & fresh fire into the dead churches and Christians who are powerless. Throughout the Bible, breath and wind represent the Holy Spirit. When the Holy Spirit breathes on you, you will suddenly come alive. The dry bones became a mighty army. The church is called be an army! We are called to be full of life and full of the Holy Spirit, marching together for God's kingdom.

God wants every dry bone to live. If you feel spiritually lost or spiritually dead, today is the day for you to come alive! God says to you, "Then you, my people, will know that I am the Lord, when I open your graves and bring you up from them. I will put my Spirit in you and you will live" (Ezekiel 37:13–14). God is in the business of raising the dead!

CHAPTER 4: ANOINTED FOR WHAT?

CHAPTER 4: ANOINTED FOR WHAT?

I n the Old Testament and New Testament alike, *the anointing* spoke of a special action by the empowerment of the Holy Spirit. The word *anointing* means, "To smear or rub with oil, typically as part of a religious ceremony"

But the anointing is more than just rubbing oil on someone; it is an impartation of an unction on one's life to cause that one to carry out assignments. David was anointed with oil by God's prophet. That was the outward expression—but what happened inwardly was far more important. The power of the Holy Spirit came upon David to equip him for the future assignment God had for him. Why does God anoint us and empower us with His Holy Spirit?

> The Spirit of the Lord is on me, because he has anointed me to proclaim good news to the poor. He has sent me to proclaim freedom for the prisoners and recovery

of sight for the blind, to set the oppressed
free, to proclaim the year of the Lord's
favor. (Luke 4:18–19)

A Kingdom of Power

Do you know what you carry? People are looking for
the power of God—but it is not a lack of power on God's
part. It is our failure to tap into the power source that He
has already given us.

In January of 2020, I was headed to the airport in
Colorado to fly back home. I was running late, and I
hadn't even checked in yet or paid for my luggage. I
arrived at the airport about forty-five minutes before
my flight boarded, so I ran to the kiosk to check in and
print my boarding pass. After I dropped my luggage at
baggage claim, I ran down to TSA and then hopped on
the train to my gate.

As I looked at my boarding pass to see the gate
number I need to go to and what my seat number was
on the plane, I was surprised to see that my seat was
right in the front of the plane. If you're late to check in,
you're pretty much going to sit in the back of the plane,
especially if it's a full flight. I was looking forward to
boarding and taking a nap until we landed.

I found my seat and got situated, and as I closed my
eyes, a lady needed to get to her seat by the window in
the same row as me. As the plane took off, she started a
conversation with me about how she was from Pakistan

and was studying to get her PhD. She started sharing her faith with me—Islam. I wanted to take a nap, but I felt in my heart that this was the reason God put me in the front of the plane. This was a divine appointment.

I started sharing the gospel of Jesus Christ with this Muslim woman, and I looked at her asked if she had any pain in her body. She replied that she had pain in her foot. I held out my hand and asked if I could pray for her. She looked down at my hand and then looked me in the eyes and told me that because I was not a close relative, I could not touch her. She genuinely wanted prayer, so she took off her scarf and put it over her hand and said, "You can pray now."

I told her I was going to pray two prayers. The first prayer would be in her god's name, and the second prayer would be in my God's name. She agreed to it, so I began praying in her god's name, and I asked her if she felt anything. After she said no, I began praying in the name of Jesus. She immediately felt heat go in her foot. After I prayed, I asked her if there was any pain left, and she said, "No, it's gone." I told her how my Bible says that the kingdom of God is not a matter of talk, but of power (1 Corinthians 4:20).

The Importance of Immediate Obedience

Paul said, "My message and my preaching were not with wise and persuasive words, but with a demonstration of the Spirit's power" (1 Corinthians 2:4). Furthermore, Acts 4:12 says, "Salvation is found in no one else [but Jesus Christ], for there is no other name under heaven given unto mankind by which we must be saved." We have to understand the power that is in the name of Jesus. Buddha said he was a teacher of truth, and Muhammad said he was a prophet of truth—but Jesus said He *is* the Truth!

If a Christian's life isn't supernatural, it's superficial.

Not only is acting without hesitation a blessing to us, but the lives of other people may depend on it. They are waiting on our immediate obedience. You are carrying someone's miracle. Don't let it stay inside. You have to release it. If a Christian's life isn't supernatural, it's superficial.

People tell me all the time, "Well, Matt, one day when I'm ready, I'll go." I tell them that your "one day" has to turn into your today! It is time to live a life worthy of the calling you have received. It is time for people to confuse you with Jesus. Our lives should be a demonstration of Him on earth. We are called to action; we are called to go. The great commission is not a great suggestion. Jesus told us to go into all the world. It is not a suggestion; it is a command. He expects us to rise up.

The church is a body of believers who live out the gospel through their words and actions. It is at its best when people *inside* the building take Jesus's message *outside* the building and serve those they meet. The great commission is too big for one to do alone, and too important for us not to try and do it together. Now is the time to start doing something with what is on the inside of you. You are a soldier in the army of God!

The great commission is not a great suggestion.

Be Full of the Holy Spirit's Power

Many Christians fear witnessing because they think they have to do it with their own natural abilities, their own persuasive power, etc. Paul says, "My message and my preaching were not with wise and persuasive words, but with a demonstration of the Spirit's power" (1 Corinthians 2:4).

> In a few days you will be baptized with the Holy Spirit. . . . You will receive power when the Holy Spirit comes on you; and you will be my witnesses in Jerusalem, and in all Judea and Samaria, and to the ends of the earth. (Acts 1:5, 8)

One purpose of the Holy Spirit's anointing which comes in the baptism with the Holy Spirit is to give us power to be Christ's witnesses. "You will receive power" indicated that those who receive the power will be His witnesses. There are no powerless Christians when they are filled with the Holy Spirit and walking in the anointing of God, having received their own personal Pentecost, just like the early disciples did in Acts chapter 2. The anointing gives you Holy Ghost power to be a good witness. When was the last time you remember being used in the anointing of God?

Jesus, the Anointed One, is the real source of our victory and freedom from bondage.

How many of our problems would be solved if we just had a fresh anointing of the Holy Spirit in our lives? We know from the Word of God that it is His will that all people are filled with the Holy Spirit. We need to be full reservoirs instead of a lake with no outlet. How full are you? How much of you does the Holy Spirit possess and control?

So many people tell me, "Matt, I just want more of God so I can do what you do." The question isn't how much more of God you can get—it's how much He has of you. The anointing of God is the Holy Spirit; He flows as a river of love from the throne of grace, through the hearts of believers, bringing life to all who receive His touch. It is time to get in His presence and receive a fresh anointing! There is an invitation for further consecration. More holiness. More fire.

You are not limited by your own lack of skills. As Jesus promised, "You will receive power." This promise enables you by the Spirit of God to minister for the Lord beyond your natural capabilities. The anointing of the Holy Spirit is given through people to demonstrate God's love and power. The name *Christ* means "Anointed One." Because Christ is in us, we have the same anointing that He had on Earth. Christ in you, the hope of glory! But you also need to abide in Him. See, if He is just in you, then you are hoping for glory; but when you are in Him, you are *living* in glory. You are in Christ for salvation, but Christ is in you for other people.

We need the power of the Holy Spirit. You cannot lead your family, make wise decisions, overcome evil, and walk in God's will without it.

We need the power of the Holy Spirit. You cannot lead your family, make wise decisions, overcome evil, and walk in God's will without it. This is why many Christians are fearful, angry, bitter, and unproductive. They aren't walking in the power of the Spirit. It's time to be full of the spirit! The ambition that God had for every human being, every person, one made in His image, is to be absolutely filled, saturated, and overflowing with this permanent river, this ongoing spring of life called the Holy Spirit of God. It is to be possessed and filled with God Himself.

Five Purposes of the Anointing

> The Spirit of the Lord is on me, because
> he has anointed me to preach good news
> to the poor. He has sent me to proclaim
> freedom for the prisoners and recovery of
> sight for the blind, to release the oppressed,
> to proclaim the year of the Lord's favor.
> (Luke 4:18–19)

In this verse, five purposes of the anointing—
five aspects of the work of the Holy Spirit in us—
are revealed:

1. To enable you to "preach the good news" effectively.
   The news we share about Jesus is good! The
   anointing will enable you to share it with impact.
2. "Proclaim freedom for the prisoners." To make you
   a Spirit-filled messenger, a proclaimer of freedom—
   freedom from the prison of sin, drugs, depression,
   and life-dominating habits.
3. You are anointed to bring "recovery of sight for
   the blind"—both physical and spiritual healing, as
   Jesus did.
4. You are anointed "to release the oppressed." All
   around you are people oppressed by sin, by sickness,
   by demonic attacks, etc. You have a message of
   release for them.

5. You are anointed "to proclaim the year of the Lord's favor" to people ignorant of the comforting message of God's grace.

> You know what has happened throughout Judea, beginning in Galilee after the baptism that John preached— how God anointed Jesus of Nazareth with the Holy Spirit and power, and how he went around doing good and healing all who were under the power of the devil, because God was with him. (Acts 10:37–38)

The Holy Spirit anointing brings to you the power of God to go around "doing good." The heaven-sent power to do good in ways even beyond our natural abilities is one of the benefits of the anointing. The anointing empowers us to be the hands and feet of Jesus. It gives you the Holy Spirit's power to break the devil's yoke in people's lives.

> But you have an anointing from the Holy One, and all of you know the truth. . . . I am writing these things to you about those who are trying to lead you astray. As for you, the anointing you received from him remains in you, and you do not need anyone to teach you. But as his anointing teaches you about all things and as that anointing is real,

> not counterfeit—just as it has taught you,
> remain in him. (1 John 2:20, 26–27)

The anointing empowers us to hear, discern, and hold to truth. You have been anointed by God with His holy oil and stamped with His stamp of approval. It is time to rise up!

CHAPTER 5:
CLOTHED WITH
POWER

Chapter 5: Clothed with Power

The Holy Spirit is our power source to live for God. We must plug into Him if we are going to live for Him. That is why Jesus promised that His followers would be baptized in the Holy Spirit. In order for us to fulfill the mission Jesus has given the church, the power and promise of the baptism of the Holy Spirit is a complete necessity. I did not start witnessing effectively until after I was empowered by the Holy Spirit. It was then that I started sharing the gospel with boldness, courage, fire, and authority.

When you received Jesus as your Savior, you were born again by the Holy Spirit. You became a temple of the Holy Spirit because He was dwelling within you. This work is referred to as the regenerating work of the Holy Spirit. But the baptism in the Holy Spirit is not the same as salvation—it is the empowering work of the Holy Spirit.

What exactly is the baptism with the Holy Spirit if it is not the same as salvation? Baptism comes after salvation. When someone is saved, the Holy Spirit places them in the body of Christ; but beyond that, Christians need to be filled with the Holy Spirit and special soul-winning power. What did Jesus teach about this baptism?

The Holy Spirit is our power source to live for God. We must plug into Him if we are going to live for Him.

On one occasion following the resurrection, the disciples were hiding away in an upper room. John records that while they were there, Jesus suddenly appeared before them bodily, and His disciples were indwelled by the Holy Spirit.

> When He had said this, He showed them His hands and His side. Then the disciples were glad when they saw the Lord. Jesus said to them again, "Peace be with you. As the Father has sent me, even so I am sending you." And when he had said this, he breathed on them and said to them, "Receive the Holy Spirit." (John 20:20–22 ESV)

This passage clearly shows that they received the Holy Spirit, but the real power was to come later. Several days later, as the disciples gathered to listen to Jesus, the

Lord gave this promise: "You will be baptized with the Holy Spirit not many days from now" (Acts 1:5 ESV). Now, if they had received the Holy Spirit earlier, then what was it that Jesus was referring to? This is what we call the baptism with the Holy Spirit, or God's power in the believer. It would not be until the day of Pentecost when the power of the Holy Spirit fell upon them—and then these fearful disciples proceeded to turn the world upside down for Christ.

Promise, Power, and Purpose

The baptism in the Holy Spirit is the fulfillment of God's promise to every believer that they would receive power to fulfill God's purpose to be witnesses. Notice the three words: *promise*, *power*, and *purpose*. It is these three words that are essential for understanding the baptism in the Holy Spirit.

Promise

The promise of the power of the Holy Spirit is for every believer. Jesus promised it both before and after His resurrection. Here is another instance when Jesus spoke about it:

> I am going to send you what my Father has promised; but stay in the city until you have been clothed with power from on high. (Luke 24:49)

Jesus demonstrated the importance of this baptism by commanding his followers to wait in Jerusalem until they received the Holy Spirit's power (see Acts 1:4). He knew they needed the indwelling Spirit in order to carry the gospel and fulfill their mission.

On the day of Pentecost, when the fulfillment of the promise happened, Peter stood before the crowd that gathered at the temple and proclaimed that what had happened was the fulfillment of the promise, which the prophet Joel had prophesied many years before:

> In the last days, God says, I will pour out my Spirit on all people. Your sons and daughters will prophesy, your young men will see visions, your old men will dream dreams. Even on my servants, both men and women, I will pour out my Spirit in those days, and they will prophesy. (Acts 2:17–18)

Peter explained that this promise was meant for every generation both present and to come. Then he said:

> Repent and be baptized, every one of you, in the name of Jesus Christ for the forgiveness of your sins. And you will receive the gift of the Holy Spirit. The promise is for you and your children and for all who are far off—for all whom the Lord our God will call. (Acts 2:38–39)

Joel envisioned—and Peter proclaimed—that it was now time for all people, regardless of age, social status, or gender, to enter into this glorious relationship with the Holy Spirit. The prophet Ezekiel also prophesied of the outpouring of the Holy Spirit:

> I will no longer hide my face from them,
> for I will pour out my Spirit on the house
> of Israel, declares the Sovereign Lord.
> (Ezekiel 39:29)

Now, today, the promise of God's Spirit is available to every believer who calls on the Lord. Every believer can be empowered by the Holy Spirit!

Power

> But you will receive power when the Holy
> Spirit comes on you. (Acts 1:8)

Jesus promises *power*. The Greek word is *dunamis*. It is where we get our word *dynamite* from. It is also translated as ability, efficiency, and might. The power of the Holy Spirit also involves courage, boldness, confidence, insight, and authority. The disciples would need all these gifts in order to fulfill their mission.

Purpose

Having power is great, but without a reason for having the power, it doesn't do any good. The first thing we need to find out is how this power is supposed to function in our lives. What is the purpose of it? Jesus said those who receive the Holy Spirit would receive power to *walk*, power to *witness*, and power to *work* miracles. It's the power to live like Jesus in our world!

First of all, it is power to *walk* like Jesus. The baptism in the Holy Spirit gives us power to emulate Him with our lives. How can we live for Jesus in this world? With the help of the Holy Spirit equipping us. With our immersion into the Holy Spirit comes an opportunity to be clothed in power from on high. Jesus prophesied to His disciples:

> For John baptized with water, but in a few days, you will be baptized with the Holy Spirit. (Acts 1:5)

And John the Baptist had said about Jesus:

> I baptize you with water for repentance. But after me comes one who is more powerful than I, whose sandals I am not worthy to carry. He will baptize you with the Holy Spirit and with fire. (Matthew 3:11)

The Greek word for *baptize* is a word that literally means to be immersed or covered over. It means to be totally submerged. The baptism in the Holy Spirit produces change; it changes our purpose and how we walk in life. Galatians 5:25 says, "Since we live by the Spirit, let us keep in step with the Spirit." It is the power of the Holy Spirit which enables believers to live for Jesus.

We receive power *to witness* for Jesus.

> You will receive power when the Holy Spirit comes on you; and you will be my witnesses. (Acts 1:8)

This is more of a promise than a command! The baptism in the Holy Spirit gives us the power to be witnesses for the Lord. The Great Commission tells us to make disciples of all nations, teaching them to obey everything He commanded us. That is why Jesus instructs us to receive the Spirit.

Power to *work miracles* of Jesus. It is power to do the things He did—and even greater ones!

> Very truly I tell you, whoever believes in me will do the works I have been doing, and they will do even greater things than these, because I am going to the Father. (John 14:12)

When Jesus had gathered His disciples together, He gave them this parting promise and commission:

> And these signs will accompany those who believe: In my name they will drive out demons; they will speak in new tongues; they will pick up snakes with their hands;

and when they drink deadly poison, it will not hurt them at all; they will place their hands on sick people, and they will get well. (Mark 16:17–18)

The baptism in the Holy Spirit is the promise of God to every believer to receive power in order to fulfill God's purpose to be His witness. The baptism in the Holy Spirit will make you effective for the kingdom. Jesus said that His followers would receive the Holy Spirit, that He would give them power, and they would witness with extraordinary results. Often we try to reverse the order and witness by our own power. But witnessing isn't showing what we can do for God. It is showing and telling what God has done for us.

Witnessing isn't showing what we can do for God. It is showing and telling what God has done for us.

God not only wants to increase your intimacy with Him, but also your spiritual *power* to minister. This baptism is not just for our personal spiritual blessing— it also *empowers* us to bless others. This how we can witness with extraordinary results. This experience is not just something that happens to you; it is something that works *through* you. Why ask for something that you will not use to bless others? All of this abounding power is available to every believer who simply asks and, in obedience, waits for God to fill them. You might be thinking, *With all this power available to every follower of Jesus, why aren't more people walking and living in the fullness of the Spirit's power?* That is a good question. I believe it is simply because people have not asked. Jesus said that we don't have things because we haven't asked. Then he says,

> For everyone who asks receives; he who seeks finds; and to him who knocks, the door will be opened. Which of you fathers, if your son asks for a fish, will give him a snake instead? Or if he asks for an egg, will give him a scorpion? If you then, though you are evil, know how to give good gifts to your children, how much more will your Father in heaven give good gifts to those who ask him! (Luke 11:10–13)

How do you receive? If you want the Lord to baptize you in the Holy Spirit today, just do a few simple things:

1. ASK

2. CONFESS

3. THANK HIM, then open your mouth and

4. SPEAK OUT

Chapter 6: How to Evangelize Effectively

CHAPTER 6: HOW TO EVANGELIZE EFFECTIVELY

Every Christian is anointed to proclaim the good news. You do not have to be a theologian to tell your neighbor, family member, or co-worker about Jesus. You don't even have to function in the office of an evangelist to evangelize. Sharing your faith and loving on people is the lifestyle of Christianity. That is what evangelism is: your relationship with God on display in public.

Let's talk about the role and function of the evangelist. I have studied this role for the past few years, and I want to share with you what I have learned. This role is the work of the ministry. The Greek word for *evangelist* means "one who announces the good news." The work of the evangelist is best defined as "Winning the lost to Christ, through the preaching of the word, in the power of the Holy Spirit, for the building up of the body of Christ." The evangelist functions within the operation of the law of sowing and reaping. He is a "reaper" in a harvest field. In 1 Corinthians 3:6, the Lord of the harvest uses the ministry of sowing (the pastors and teachers) and the ministry of reaping (the role of the evangelist). I have learned that there are seasons of sowing and reaping within every church. To sow but never harvest is a disaster, while to reap where there has been no sowing brings a poor harvest. — Discern The Time

The Work of an Evangelist

So what exactly does an evangelist do? In past church history, the task of witnessing to the lost was mainly heaped onto the shoulders of those who operate in the office of the evangelist, but if you look carefully at the Greek meaning and historical culture for those who were called "evangelists," you may be surprised at what you will find. These "evangelists" were sent to the army troops positioned all over the country. Their job was to go to those soldiers and proclaim good news about what their king was saying and doing to get the troops pumped up and ready to go out into battle. This falls right in line with what we read about the ministry gifts and what those who are called to one of those fivefold ministry offices are supposed to be doing: building up the body of Christ:

> So Christ himself gave the apostles, the
> prophets, the evangelists, the pastors and
> teachers, to equip his people for works

86

of service, so that the body of Christ may be built up until we all reach unity in the faith and in the knowledge of the Son of God and become mature, attaining to the whole measure of the fullness of Christ. (Ephesians 4:11-13)

So the evangelist comes in to build up everyone in the church to go out and do the work of the ministry! All along, we have been passing off the job of witnessing to the lost to those who hold the office of the evangelist, when their main purpose is to build the church up to go out and win the lost. In the sense that we think of evangelism in terms of winning the lost, we are all supposed to be doing that work.

The evangelist comes in to build up everyone in the church to go out and do the work of the ministry!

This is why Paul encourages Timothy to always be ready to share his faith:

Preach the word; be prepared in season and out of season; correct, rebuke and encourage—with great patience and careful instruction. (2 Timothy 4:2)

As a follower of Jesus, we have to always be ready to know what we believe and why we believe it. If someone asked you today how you know God is real and what they need to do to be saved, would you be ready with an answer? Would you know the right scriptures to either quote or find easily to point them to Jesus—even if they were debating with you about your beliefs? If you aren't sure, then part of your job as a believer is to get ready for whenever that opportunity may arise. We need to be prepared to turn "an out of season" into an "In season" opportunity. Make it a point to study salvation scriptures and read books (like this one) about evangelism and sharing your faith.

Look for the Opportunity

Some people may say, "Matt, nobody ever talks to me about Jesus. How am I supposed to share my faith if the subject never comes up?" Maybe the reason some people aren't ready is because they are not actively looking for opportunities to spread the good news. There are opportunities every day to talk to people around us about Jesus—sometimes we aren't actually looking for them or hoping someone else will do it, so we don't have to.

When was the last time you were with someone who said they were having a bad day, or that they had some problem at home, or were dealing with a health issue of some sort? I would guess it happens fairly often. Those conversations can turn into a golden moment that allows us to speak life into those situations. If anything, just asking if they mind if you pray for them might be the very thing they need to build their hope and believe for their miracle, thus being a step closer to coming to Jesus.

Part of the problem with the generation and culture we live in is that we get so busy, distracted, or inwardly focused when we are around other people that we fail to pay attention to the people around us when we are in their presence. How many hurting people have been sitting or standing right next to us, and we had our face buried in our phones? We need to be asking the Lord who might be around us to minister to and then listen to the Holy Spirit's voice nudging us in the right direction. One thing I love about the ministry of the Holy Spirit, is that He directs and arranges the meeting between the sinner and the soul winner. Even between one who has gone astray, and one who is walking with the Lord. Most of the time, we are not sensitive to this kind of leading or prompting by the Holy Spirit mainly due to fear, lack of zeal to win a soul, and being discouraged by our personal challenges, but the truth is that the Holy Spirit is still making such arrangements today! The world is depending on us!

Get Over Your Fears

Another main reason we don't share Jesus with others is because of fear; fear that we won't know what to say, fear that we will sound stupid, and fear of rejection. It's been said many times before, but it's worth bringing up now: If Jesus was publicly humiliated for us, we shouldn't care about what other people think of us when we are working for Him.

We get over our fear of not knowing what to say by being ready. Study the Word; know your Bible! Not only will it build up your own spirit, but it will also help you be prepared whenever you see a chance to minister to someone.

We get over our fear of sounding stupid by actually sharing our faith with people. The more you talk with people about the Lord, the easier it will become. Don't let this stop you from witnessing to others. Sure, you may say something dumb now and then, but if your heart is right, God can still use it.

We get over our fear of rejection by being secure in our identity in Christ. When we really grasp that we are God's children—sons and daughters of the most high God; heirs to the kingdom—we won't care what people think about us. And in that identity comes compassion for the lost because we will realize on an even greater level how much they really need Jesus and how much our Savior truly loves them and doesn't want them to perish. Out of knowing who you are in Christ, you become infected with love for the lost—which then allows you to start bleeding for the lost.

Once we get over these fears and start looking for opportunities, we may be shocked at how often we are witnessing to people around us. God's Word is always relevant to any culture and each generation, so once we open our eyes, we will see a whole world of hurting people—a field that is ripe for harvest (see John 4:35-38).

Focus on Your Relationship with Jesus

You will never lead people to where you are not. In other words, if you are not close with Jesus, you are not going to lead anyone there. Not only will we lead people to the wrong place, but it comes off as fake. Would you trust the words of a salesperson who doesn't use the product they are selling? Probably not, because it's not genuine; they just want a paycheck. That is how many Christians come off. They aren't really interested in Jesus, at least not enough to change their actions. If you want to see Jesus change lives through you, you have to first pour into your relationship with Him. Otherwise, what you do will be ineffective and come off as disingenuous. Evangelizing effectively means getting closer to Jesus yourself.

How to Evangelize

Our culture is changing, and our evangelism needs to change with it. Methods that once worked will increasingly become ineffective. The message will always remain the same, but the method needs to change.

When I see people downtown with big signs lifted high yelling, "Jesus or hell! Repent or burn!" I cringe inside and my heart is grieved—because that is ineffective. Although it is 100% true, it is incomplete.

Jesus said, "By this everyone will know that you are my disciples, if you love one another" (John 13:35).

People may hate us because of Jesus, but they should never hate Jesus because of us.

Our love should make non-believers question their disbelief in God. A major problem with many believers who witness is that they try clean the fish before they even catch the fish. We have to love and meet people where they are. Our job is to love others without stopping to inquire whether or not they are worthy. People may hate us because of Jesus, but they should never hate Jesus because of us. I heard someone say that the way we treat others should lead them to only one conclusion: "If this is how Jesus loves, then I'm in." Let your love for God change the world, but never let the world change your love for God.

When we talk about how to share the gospel, it is important to understand what the gospel is. It is not your personal testimony. It isn't sharing a random scripture. It isn't an apologetic debate. Neither is it a heated argument over theology. The gospel is an announcement, not an argument; you share it, not shove it. The gospel is simply the good news about the life, death, burial, and resurrection of Christ. Our stories are not the gospel, but they can incorporate this good news. Every believer should be ready in season and out of season to share what God has done in his or her life. You have never truly found Jesus unless you tell others about Him. If you tell *your* story—what God is doing in your own life—no one can argue with you. Your feelings and experiences are your own, and no one can debate them. Many people may be resistant to hearing any bible stories, but they are more likely to be interested in a personal transformation story. Salvation belongs to the Lord. The Word of God clearly teaches us that while we are responsible for planting and watering, only God can produce the fruit. Paul explained to the believers in Corinth: "So neither the one who plants nor the one who waters is anything, but only God, makes things grow" (1 Corinthians 3:7). It is not our responsibility for others to accept the truth, but we are called to ensure that they have a chance to accept it. It doesn't matter if they reject you, because the seed you plant speaks louder than their ignorance!

The gospel is an announcement, not an argument; you share it, not shove it.

Whenever you get rejected, be encouraged; Jesus says in Luke 10:16, "Whoever listens to you listens to me; whoever rejects you rejects me; but whoever rejects me rejects him who sent me." Whenever someone rejects me while trying to minister to them, I pray that God will send the right people to minister to them in a way that they would listen and understand. I ask God to open their heart to believe. I approach God confidently in this way: God loves them even more than we do, and His will is for all people to be saved and come to the knowledge of the truth. (See 1 Timothy 2:4). Scripture tells us that no one comes to God unless the Father draws them, so it makes sense to ask God to draw them to Himself and open their hearts to believe. In the book of Acts, a religious woman named Lydia was trying to worship God the best way she knew how. But she hadn't trusted Jesus as her Savior. Paul shared the gospel with her, just like we should do with unbelievers. And then something miraculous happened. Acts 16:14 describes it in this way: "The Lord opened her heart to respond to Paul's message."

Here are the three keys I use to evangelize effectively:

1. Give a brief description of what your life was like before you received Christ.
2. Describe how God spoke to your heart and opened your eyes to spiritual truth. Include the basic facts of the gospel and your response of faith.
3. Finally, share how your life has changed since receiving the forgiveness available in Christ.

When it comes to initiating a conversation, there needs to be an ice breaker. The best way to start a conversation with someone is to break the ice and ask them their name, where they're from, talk about the weather, or anything that will get their attention. After breaking the ice, use a conversation starter into the gospel message. Here is a list of conversation starters I use when interacting with people:

- Are you a believer?
- Do you know how to have a relationship with God?
- Did you grow up in church? What were you taught about God growing up? Do you still believe that?
- May I pray for you? Do you have any special needs I can pray for?
- What do you think the solution to (insert recent troubling news event) is?
- Do you have time for a short story? It's the greatest thing that's ever happened to me, and I love to tell people about it!
- What did you think of the pastor's message this week? (After attending a church service.)

CHAPTER 7: CULTIVATING A HEART ON FIRE

CHAPTER 7:
CULTIVATING A HEART
ON FIRE

I f you have ever gone camping, you will know how important fire is, especially in the evening. During the first camping experience I ever had, I learned just a few hours into the evening how important fire is to campers. We cook our food with it, keep warm with it, and use it to provide light.

If you are camping in the middle of the woods or near a lake, the last thing you want to happen in the evening is for your fire to go out. In one way or another, we believers are like campers in the dark, in need of the light and warmth of a heart steadily on fire for God. 2 Timothy 1:6 says:

> For this reason I remind you to fan into flame the gift of God, which is in you through the laying on of my hands, for

God gave us a spirit not of fear but of
power and love and self-control. (ESV)

In this scripture, Paul speaks to young Timothy
with regards to guarding the deposit of the message
of Christ. I believe that if we want to sustain the hope
made available through Christ, we need to keep that fire
burning inside of us.

A few summers ago, I went camping with my friend
and his family. Every night after dinner, everyone would
meet by the bonfire for s'mores and fellowship. Every
time the flame would start to dim, I and someone else
would go to the side of the cabin where there was a pile
of wood specifically for the bonfire. We grabbed fresh
food and brought it to the pit. As long as wood was on
the fire, we could be assured that we would have heat.
But if there was no wood left to burn or if only embers
were left, it was certain that the fire would go out unless
we took action. You see, fuel was essential to keep the
fire going—and when fuel of any sort is depleted, the fire
eventually goes out.

During that trip, there was enough wood to keep the
fire burning, but it needed to be stoked—meaning that
it needed to be moved around and repositioned. In fact,
if we didn't regularly stoke those embers and fan the
flames, we discovered that the fire could go out, even if
there was enough wood to keep it burning. Those embers
had to be tended to regularly in order to keep the fire

going strong. In the same way, we need to stoke our hearts regularly to keep our spiritual flame alive.

I want to share some keys that I have learned for keeping that fire for God burning passionately through the darkness that we walk through in our lifetimes.

Never Neglect the Word

No matter how much we grow, no one ever outgrows the basics of God's Word and prayer. Psalm 119:105 tells us, "Your word is a lamp to my feet and a light to my path" (ESV). Throughout all the seasons of life, communication with God is vitally important for keeping that passion for Him burning. The primary way we communicate with God is through prayer, and He also speaks to us through His Word.

No matter how much we grow, no one ever outgrows the basics of God's Word and prayer.

A Heart of Thanksgiving

Whenever I sense that the fire has gone out and my passion has waned, it's *almost always* because I stopped being grateful—stopped thanking God for everything He has done, and all of the blessings I enjoy. I've learned that when we focus too much on what we don't have and on what God is not giving us at the moment, we lose sight of the fact that God is always wonderfully good, is for us, and will never forsake us. Start today by thanking Him for everything you'd miss tomorrow if you woke up and it wasn't there.

> Give thanks in all circumstances; for this is God's will for you in Christ Jesus. (1 Thessalonians 5:18)

Repentance

I believe sin and selfish attitudes are fire-quenchers. Scripture says that His kindness leads us to repentance. When you have spent some time thanking God, conviction returns to your soul.

Keep it Real

First you have to be honest with yourself; we call it "keeping it real." When you start to feel guilt and remorse about something you have done or something going on in your life, you have to be honest about it. If you have issues that are affecting your relationship with Christ, quit making excuses. It's your fault—not someone else's.

King David had a "keeping-it-real" moment in Psalm 51:1–3, and when he did, he cried to the Lord, "Have mercy on me, O God, according to your unfailing love; according to your great compassion, blot out my transgressions. Wash away all my iniquity and cleanse me from my sin. For I know my transgressions, and my sin is always before me."

Are you ready to be honest? Are you ready to come out of denial? Are you ready to start keeping it real? If you are, then you are ready for repentance.

Repentance

After we feel all this guilt and remorse being lifted away from us after repentance, then we begin renewal. We start to renew that relationship with our Savior, we start renewing those relationships with our friends and family, and we begin anew with those we love. Repentance is the forerunner to revival. Living a lifestyle of repentance is vital to keeping that fire burning in our hearts.

Now I want to show you what I have learned for how you can avoid falling back into that same old routine.

Replacement

One word: *Replacement*. When we get rid of sin, we must put on Christ. Replace those bad habits with good ones. Put off your old self and put on the new; turn from destructive to constructive.

Jesus told a story in Matthew 12:43–45 about replacing the old with something new. He had just cast out a demon, and the demon had to find a new home. So while it was wandering around, the demon came upon its old residence all cleaned up, but empty. So the demon found seven friends more wicked than itself, and they took up residence in the man—and then he is worse off than when he started. It is more than just cleaning house; you have to fill it with something better. You have to fill it with the Holy Spirit. If not, you will fall back into the same old ways with a little more bad added to it.

What's Next?

Repentance and faith are linked in Scripture. Repentance means turning from sin, and faith means turning to God. John the Baptist and the apostle Paul urged people to turn to the Scriptures, and they urge us to turn to the Word today. The Scriptures give us strength, courage, and wisdom to persevere in our walk of faith. Take the next step and dare to say, "Search me, God, and know my heart; test me and know my anxious thoughts. See if there is any offensive way in me, and lead me in the way everlasting" (Psalm 139:23–24).

Confession is a cleansing, beautiful thing. God draws especially near to the humble, repentant heart.

> Therefore confess your sins to each other and pray for each other so that you may be healed. The prayer of a righteous person is powerful and effective. (James 5:16)

So many people allow guilt and condemnation to drown out the revelation of the power of the blood of Jesus. See, there is a difference between condemnation and conviction. Condemnation causes shame; conviction causes repentance. I have learned that the Holy Spirit convicts us for the purpose of restoration, and the devil condemns us for the purpose of separation. We need to live a lifestyle of repentance if we want this fire to be burning passionately in our hearts.

When we feel our flame flickering and not burning brightly, it is often because we have approached God only for what He can do for us and not for who He is. A sure way to fan our spiritual flame is to seek Him for all He is worth. Still bring your requests before Him, but then lay them down at His feet and seek to know His heart. He is the star-breathing God, the Lord of Lords, the King of Kings, and the God of angel armies! He is high and lifted up, and yet intimately right here. He loves you. Get to know Him in a greater capacity, and you will have a better understanding of how He is working in your current circumstances. To better know Him is to love Him more, and to know Him is to be filled to the fullness with Him. The more you know Him and commune with Him, the more the Spirit will make you like Him.

> The fear of the Lord is the beginning of
> wisdom, and knowledge of the Holy One
> is understanding. (Proverbs 9:10)

Stand firm

When we don't feel like praying or stirring up the gift of God within us, when it feels like His promises don't exactly feel true, it is time to stand on the Word of God because it *is* true. When I find myself feeling more earthbound than heaven-bound, I rise up, walk around my room, and proclaim the promises of God written over my life. Doing this will stoke your spiritual flame. Declare that you are who God says you are, that worry is not your master, you are significant, you are empowered and filled with purpose. You will not die, but live, and declare the works of the Lord. God's grace abounds in your life so you can abound in every good work!

When you stand on God's promises and your ears hear your mouth say what is true, a fresh fire is ignited in your heart. I challenge you to walk around, stomp your feet (if you have to), and proclaim the promises of God. Take your stand—right where you stand!

> For you have exalted above all things your
> name and your word. (Psalm 138:2 ESV)

Here are some ways that we can stay standing strong in our faith and not get loose that Holy fire.

Remain in Fellowship

I read something one time that said when a burning coal is removed from a pile of red-hot coals, it loses its fire as it sits alone. We Christians experience the same thing. That is why church community and fellowship are' vital to our everyday walk. When we stay within accountability, encouragement, and discipleship that comes through fellowship, we remain on fire for God. The bible says iron sharpens iron!

Remember the Joy of Your Salvation

When David felt his fire for God dying, which led to his immorality with Bathsheba, he cried out to God, saying, "Cast me not away from your presence, and take not your Holy Spirit from me. Restore to me the joy of your salvation, and uphold me with a willing spirit" (Psalm 51:11–12 ESV).

Do you remember the first time you received Jesus into your life, and the joy that came right after? That joy wasn't meant to be experienced one time, we can and should walk in it every day!

Go Back to Your First Love

Revelation 2:4 speaks of the first love that has been abandoned so many times. Our first love is and always will be Jesus! What keeps us focused on Christ as our first love is this great reminder that it was He who loved us first, and our love for Him comes simply as a response to the greatest love we will ever know. Paul told Timothy to passionately and rigorously begin again to stoke and stir up the gift of God in his life, just as one would stoke the embers of a fire in a fireplace. Paul was not just kindly suggesting that Timothy take action; he was

GOD'S INVITATION TO YOU

commanding him to reach within spiritually and begin to rekindle the fire in his heart.

I encourage you to reach within your own heart and begin to spiritually rekindle the fire inside of you. At the time Paul wrote to Timothy, this young man was surrounded by confusion resulting from the intense persecution that was taking place. Is it possible that he was exhausted and that his own fire was beginning to wane? Most likely, the answer is yes.

Regardless of what Timothy was going through, Paul told him to take action before the fire in his heart went out. Timothy was to open the door to his heart, look inside to determine the condition of his inward fire, and then take action to "put more wood on the fire" and stir up the gift of God inside him. If Timothy would obey Paul's command, that inward fire would blaze again. It is the same for you. If your "fire" is at a low burn or close to going out, it is time for you to take Paul's words to heart "to stir up" the gift of God that is inside you. You cannot depend on someone else to do something so vital for you, so ask the Holy Spirit how to do it—how to open the door to your heart and take an honest look on the inside to assess your need. Then let Him show you how to proceed in fueling your fire and stirring up those embers so that you will once again become a bright blazing inferno for Jesus Christ!

Confessions:

Lord, I confess that I need to stir up the gift of God that is in me. There was a time when it seemed the fires burned much brighter, but for one reason or another, I've allowed the flame in my spirit to grow colder. I take responsibility for this; it is my heart, and I ask You to forgive me for letting myself go this far. Today I accept responsibility, and I will look at my heart and determine the truth. With the help of the Holy Spirit, I will begin to actively and vigorously rekindle that glorious spiritual fire that You intended to burn inside me. Help me, Holy Spirit, to do this not just once, but to continually put spiritual fuel into my heart and stoke the embers.

I pray this in Jesus's name!

I confess that it is God's will for my heart to be spiritually ablaze, and today I will begin to do what I must do to rekindle the flame to burn as it once did and to blaze even brighter. I will not allow distractions— whether they come from my own busy schedule, from others, or even from myself—to take my attention off my spiritual condition ever again. I recognize that my failure to tend to the fire has affected me, and I declare that from this moment onward, I will dutifully stoke the fire and the gifts of God that have been placed inside me. I will find fuel for the fire and will take responsibility to make certain it is placed on the hearth of my heart regularly so that the fire burns bright continuously. I declare this by faith in Jesus's name!

Some Questions for You:

Can you remember a time when your heart was literally "ablaze" with the things of God? What happened along the way to affect that fire? Have you ever stopped to ponder what you could have done differently to keep it burning, regardless of the events that were happening around you?

What is your source of spiritual fuel? What feeds you? What keeps your heart on track and ablaze? Take a few minutes to write down the sources that regularly feed your heart and keep you stirred up as you serve Jesus.

How long has it been since you paused long enough to really look inside the door of your heart to see how much fuel is still there? Do you spend time with God daily and allow the Holy Spirit to do an inventory of your spiritual condition? If not, why not? This is important enough that you should start doing it every day.

CHAPTER 8: THE FULL ARMOR OF GOD

CHAPTER 8: THE FULL ARMOR OF GOD

I f you are going to be in ministry for the Lord, know that you will experience spiritual warfare. It is inevitable. We are fighting unseen enemies that will try to hinder us from fulfilling God's plan for our lives. But you need to understand that we're not alone and that we have power. We have supernatural protection for a supernatural fight. You and I will have to purposely and deliberately put on the full armor of God. When we do this, we are showing our enemy, Satan, that we are ready to stand against any tricks, schemes, or deception that he tries to bring our way, and we do this through the power of Jesus Christ and by being clothed with the armor of God.

Here is how you purposely put on your war clothes when you engage in spiritual warfare (because that is exactly what this is). When you wake up in the morning, get dressed. Let's take a look at what the Word of God says about our armor.

Finally, be strong in the Lord and in his mighty power. Put on the full armor of God, so that you can take your stand against the devil's schemes. For our struggle is not against flesh and blood, but against the rulers, against the authorities, against the powers of this dark world and against the spiritual forces of evil in the heavenly realms.

Therefore put on the full armor of God, so that when the day of evil comes, you may be able to stand your ground, and after you have done everything, to stand. Stand firm then, with the belt of truth buckled around your waist, with the breastplate of righteousness in place, and with your feet fitted with the readiness that comes from the gospel of peace. In addition to all this, take up the shield of faith, with which you can extinguish all the flaming arrows of the evil one. Take the helmet of salvation and the sword of the Spirit, which is the word of God. And pray in the Spirit on all occasions with all kinds of prayers and requests. With this in mind, be alert and always keep on praying for all the Lord's people. (Ephesians 6:10–18)

The only thing that separates the believer from the rest is that the believer fights in the army of God. The sad reality is that every person who does not faithfully serve God automatically falls under the control of the powers of darkness and is an active member in the army of the enemy.

The War Is Real

The passage above from Ephesians 6 tells us that we do not battle against "flesh and blood." This lets us know very clearly that we are not battling against people, governments, religious institutions, or political parties.

The war happening is not a war with borders or countries. It's not something that we can detect with our human senses; if it were, then the war wouldn't be so difficult. I say that this war is very difficult because the majority of people in this world are considered visual; in other words, they have to see to believe. Most people are like Thomas. They need to see it, touch it, and smell it before they can believe that it is truly real. If they can't see it, then it doesn't exist. If you think this way, then Paul's warning and most of the things contained in the Bible are of no use to you. Why? Because you can't see past the natural realm into the spiritual realm. You can't see the demons that exist, and at times surround you. And because you can't see them, you can't believe.

Just because we can't see Jesus doesn't mean that He's not there or that He abandoned us. Christ did not abandon us; the only thing He abandoned was a grave.

He didn't leave us at the mercy of our enemy. Christ left us weapons that we are to use to engage this war—He left us a complete arsenal.

Christ left us weapons that we are to use to engage this war— He left us a complete arsenal.

Take a look at everything we've been given when we read verses 13–18 again:

> Therefore put on the full armor of God, so that when the day of evil comes, you may be able to stand your ground, and after you have done everything, to stand. Stand firm then, with the belt of truth buckled around your waist, with the breastplate of righteousness in place, and with your feet fitted with the readiness that comes from the gospel of peace. In addition to all this, take up the shield of faith, with which you can extinguish all the flaming arrows of the evil one. Take the helmet of salvation and the sword of the Spirit, which is the word of God. And pray in the Spirit on all occasions with all kinds of prayers and requests. With this in mind, be alert and always keep on praying for all the Lord's people.

We have to dress correctly. Unfortunately, many fail to wear their armor on a daily basis, and the main reason for this is because many do not understand its significance. God doesn't send us into confusion, but prepares us ahead of time so that we can stand. All of the advantages of this war are in our favor. God protects us from blind attacks and prepares us for victory.

Understanding the Armor

Let's examine our weapons a little closer and see how we can use them.

The Belt of Truth

The first part of the armor is the belt; this is what is being referred to here when we read, "Stand firm then, with the belt of truth buckled around your waist." Many may see this and think that this could never be an essential part of the armor, but in reality, this piece is perhaps the most important of them all.

I want to share with you everything I've studied regarding the armor of God. The belt that the Roman soldiers used was the piece that held it all together. The belt held everything in place, and it was from there that they hung their weapons for battle. What will help us keep our breastplate in place is the *truth*. The devil is a liar, and the only way that we will be able to defeat him in battle is to do it with the truth.

Truth is the foundation on which everything is built. If you don't know what is true, you cannot avoid deception and will fall to the "wiles," or deception, of the devil. Everything in our spiritual life is fastened and held in place by truth. I've learned that without a solid understanding of truth, all defenses are compromised.

John 8:32 says, "Then you will know the truth, and the truth will set you free." When we live in truth and the sanctity of His Word, we will be able to keep the rest of the armor in place.

The Breastplate of Righteousness

The second piece of our armor is the breastplate. Scripture calls it "the breastplate of righteousness." As I was studying the armor worn by the soldiers of that time, I read that it was a piece typically made of heavy leather, and in some instances, it was reinforced with pieces of metal. This piece covered the soldier from his neck down to the waist. In other words, this piece was designed to protect the soldier's vital organs. So a soldier wearing this breastplate into battle was better protected because this piece would deflect or prevent weapons from injuring him. Our breastplate is activated when we remain faithful and pure before God.

Our breastplate is properly placed when we tear from our heart all impure feelings and erase all impure thoughts from our mind. Our breastplate is reinforced when we do away with sin and the sinful nature of this world and allow the Holy Spirit of God to guide our every step.

Shoes of the Gospel of Peace

The third piece of our armor is the footwear. Look carefully at what the scripture tells us here: "And with your feet fitted with the readiness that comes from the gospel of peace."

If we were to look at the footwear of the Roman soldier of that time, we would discover that they used sandals made out of heavy leather. But not only this; these sandals oftentimes had metal spikes on the soles so they could also be used as a weapon, not to mention that the spikes provided the soldier better stability in the battlefield, regardless of the condition of the terrain.

When we study the Scriptures, it is impossible to miss that God calls His people to stand. God calls His people to take a stand, and to stand firmly on the truth of His Word. This is why our footwear is so important—the gospel of peace. I'm talking about the peace that all of us who serve God feel regardless of the situation or circumstance. It is the peace described in Philippians 4:7: "And the peace of God, which transcends all understanding, will guard your hearts and your minds in Christ Jesus." If you don't feel this peace, then it will not be very difficult for the enemy to lay spikes in your path. It will not be difficult for the enemy to lay the broken glass of discouragement! If we aren't wearing the peace that Christ delivered unto us, then our spiritual feet will be bare, and we will be unable to stand firmly on our ground.

The Shield of Faith

The fourth piece of the armor is the shield of faith. The scripture here tells us, "In addition to all this, take up the shield of faith, with which you can extinguish all the flaming arrows of the evil one."

Let's look back at the Roman soldier's armor again, and we will discover that the shield was, in most cases, made out of wood, covered with thick leather, measuring approximately four feet high.

The soldier would make great use of this weapon and would move it from side to side to protect him during battle. Friend, the shield that we can use to protect ourselves from the attacks of the enemy is our faith. This means that the enemy will try to attack in the area of our life that might be the weakest. If our faith isn't at the appropriate level, and if we aren't taking the time to reinforce it, then it would be just like a soldier coming into battle with a paper shield. This may sound absurd, but the grim reality is that many believers don't take time to feed their faith. The more you feed your faith, the more clearly you can identify the attacks of the enemy and engage with Him properly.

Listen, you can't control what you feel, but you can control what you feed! What you feed will grow. You may be asking, "How do we feed our faith, Matt?" We feed our faith by listening to the messages that He sends us. Our faith is fed by the Word of God. Without this, our faith will wither and eventually fail.

The Helmet of Salvation

The fifth piece of our armor is the helmet. The scriptures here tell us to "take the helmet of salvation." If we had to define spiritual warfare in simple terms, we would do it by saying that it is the battle for our mind. This piece of equipment is one that can never be left behind. This piece of equipment can never be misplaced or ignored because it is the one that covers our head.

The helmet covers the area of our body where our thoughts and feelings are born. As I said, the devil knows very well that if he can control the way we think, he will be able to manipulate us to act the way he wants us to act. He will be able to manipulate us to act in a way that will separate us from God. The helmet of salvation is the knowledge that we are saved by grace and the perseverance in our faith. If we fail to persevere in our faith and if we allow our thoughts to be influenced, then we will fall wounded or even dead in the battlefield.

The Sword of the Spirit

A great reality about war is that an army will never be able to win a battle with only defensive weapons. A successful army needs defensive weapons, but they need offensive ones as well. We have the two most powerful offensive weapons that exist in the universe—and the only two that will drive the army of the enemy into a complete retreat. The scripture here tells us to take up "the sword of the Spirit, which is the word of God."

Our first offensive weapon is the Word of God. This is the only weapon that we can use to attack the frontline of the enemy. In Hebrews 4:12 we read, "For the word of God is alive and active. Sharper than any double-edged sword, it penetrates even to dividing soul and spirit, joints and marrow; it judges the thoughts and attitudes of the heart." The Word of God is penetrating; the Word of God cuts; the Word of God clears our thoughts; and the Word of God cleans our entire being.

> **Our first offensive weapon is the Word of God. This is the only weapon that we can use to attack the frontline of the enemy.**

Prayer Bombs

While studying our armor, I learned that the Word of God is like a machine gun in our arsenal, but an army just can't win with only machine guns; an army needs bombs, as well. But do we have bombs in our arsenal? Absolutely—our bombs are our prayers! Paul said it this way: "And pray in the Spirit on all occasions with all kinds of prayers and requests. With this in mind, be alert and always keep on praying for all the Lord's people" (Ephesians 6:18).

Prayer is our bomb because prayer opens the door for God's power to manifest. There is absolutely nothing impossible for Him. Jesus said it this way in Luke 1:37: "For nothing will be impossible with God" (ESV). Let's never forget that Moses prayed, and the Red Sea parted. Let's never forget that Joshua prayed, and the walls of Jericho tumbled down. Let's never forget that Elijah prayed, and fire descended from heaven. There can be no substitute for prayer, especially if we find ourselves in a difficult situation. Let's never forget what Jesus tells us in John 14:13: "Whatever you ask in my name, this I will do, that the Father may be glorified in the Son. If you ask me anything in my name, I will do it" (ESV).

There are many believers today who cannot understand that one of the most important weapons we have is the power of prayer. Yes, it's true that we must stand and advance, but the most difficult battles are not won on our feet; they are won on our knees. The most difficult battles can only be won through prayer. The spiritual war, the war for our mind, is something very real. We have to recognize that we are in a war that cannot be seen with our human eyes or detected by our human senses. We have to be very alert to all of those things that, at the time, seem insignificant or unimportant. I've learned that we can't just see things with our human eyes, but rather we look at them with our spiritual eyes as well. I heard man of God once say, "Eyes that *look* are common; eyes that *see* are rare."

One of the most important weapons we have is the power of prayer

The things that appear to be insignificant or unimportant tend to grow and grow until they separate us from the presence of God. The Word of God is never changing, and the final victory is drawing near! This is clearly stated in Revelation 20:10:

> And the devil, who deceived them, was thrown into the lake of burning sulfur, where the beast and the false prophet had been thrown. They will be tormented day and night for ever and ever.

But while we wait for this final victory, we must be winning the battles. The only way that we will ensure that this happens is by using all of the weapons that have been provided to us. Now look carefully at how you are dressed. Never forget to put on the whole armor of God, and always use the weapons you have been given. The power to win the battle is yours! If you obey and are prepared by putting on the whole armor, and you trust God's complete plan beyond what you can see, you will stand strong and your faith in God's purposes will quench what the devil attempts to use—to draw you away or create doubt.

Salvation is not found in deeds or good works; it only comes by receiving God's gift of grace. To believe in God and to believe Jesus died for your sins is only half the picture. There must be a point in time when you reach out and take God's free gift. To receive salvation, there must be a submission to Christ. When you recognize that your ways cannot make you right before God, you turn from your own ways and choose God's way. Contrary to the popular belief, it is a complete surrender. Salvation is not received at the convenience of breaking away from your lifestyle, getting salvation, and then going back to your old ways.

It is also a change of citizenship. You surrender your sinful life in exchange for the righteous life that God has prepared for you. The lifestyle you choose represents your citizenship. If you confess to have faith in Christ and then refuse to transfer your citizenship out of the world, you have not surrendered.

In conclusion, consider 1 John 1:6–7:

> If we claim to have fellowship with him and yet walk in the darkness, we lie and do not live out the truth. But if we walk in the light, as he is in the light, we have fellowship with one another, and the blood of Jesus, his Son, purifies us from all sin.

CHAPTER 9:
RADICAL DEVOTION

CHAPTER 9: RADICAL DEVOTION

God is closer than our skin, and we are often unaware of His presence. When we don't sense God is there, it is not because He's absent. It is because we have not developed a deep awareness of His presence. Everyday of our lives, we experience awareness.

When we wake up in the morning, we become aware of our surroundings and the thoughts we have. As we go throughout the day, we're aware of thousands of things. An image on the TV, a barking dog, a person's voice, an itch on your arm, a desire to drink some water, etc.

Our awareness changes from one thing to another all day long. I have learned that awareness is not a belief about something; it is directly experiencing something, whether by sight, sound, touch, taste, or consciousness. So what is the "awareness of God's presence?" It is having a consciousness of God's presence.

It is becoming aware of the presence that is here now. I remember reading a blog about the different things in our lives that affect our sensitivity to the presence of God, and one thing that stood out to me was this: "Our task is not so much to "seek love," but rather work to remove the barriers that keep us from experiencing love." I'll talk more about that in a bit. God has a deep desire to be in fellowship with us, and there's a hunger in the human soul for a relationship with Him. There is a void in us that was only created for God to fill.

What I find interesting is that God always pursues us. He always takes the initiative by His grace and seeks to draw us back into a personal friendship. So many fall short and hide from God for days until they feel as though God isn't mad at them anymore. We have to get rid of this false pattern of thinking. Friend, there could 1,000 steps between you and God, and He will take 999 of those steps and leave the last one for you. That step is repentance. Proverbs 24:16 says that though the righteous fall seven times, they rise again! God doesn't measure how many times you fall; He measures how many times you get back up. The problem is that our language and thinking can distort the process of perceiving Him. God is already present; it is we who need to be awakened to God's presence. The biblical truth and comfort we must remember is that God is always with us!

Biblical Experiences

King David acknowledged that God knew everything about him (see Psalm 139:1–5). For the person who attempts to run from God, this is convicting. He knows *everything*. There is no hiding from God! Imagine your mind as a theater screen in front of an audience of one man: Jesus. But for David, who sought God's presence, it gave him true peace. He confessed:

> Where can I go from your Spirit? Where can I flee from your presence? If I go up to the heavens, you are there; if I make my bed in the depths, you are there. If I rise on the wings of the dawn, if I settle on the far side of the sea, even there your hand will guide me, your right hand will hold me fast. (Psalm 139:7–10)

David was renewed by the truth that God guided and provided for him.

In Luke 10:38–42, Mary provides another helpful example of noticing Jesus. Martha had invited Jesus and His disciples to dinner. Although Martha's intentions of hospitality were good, she became distracted and focused on her preparations rather than on Jesus. Mary's response was different; as she "sat at the Lord's feet listening to what he said," the posture of her heart to be receptive displayed the proper attitude of a disciple to the disciple's teacher. When Martha asked Jesus to rebuke her sister and have her join her in the preparations, He gently rebuked Martha.

This passage doesn't teach that Jesus values silence over service. But Martha's anxiety about all of these preparations prevented her from enjoying Jesus's presence like Mary did. He clarified this by saying, "Few things are needed— or indeed only one. Mary has chosen what is better, and it will not be taken away from her" (v. 42). Martha was inattentive to Jesus's true needs and desire for His visit.

Friend, this verse is an example to us that our pace can radically reduce our awareness of Jesus, even though He is among us. Through different activities, we can consciously or unconsciously lose our awareness of God's presence. I was studying Exodus chapter 33 and some of the most frightening words in the Bible are found in verse 1–3, where God gave the children of Israel His protection, provision, and His promise, but not His presence.

Moses was upon Mt. Sinai to receive the Ten Commandments from the Lord. While Moses was gone, his brother Aaron led the people in rebellion against God. The people gave Aaron their bracelets and earrings, out of which Aaron made a golden calf that the people worshiped (see Exodus 32:4–10). Due to their sin, the Lord decided to remove His presence from them. He would give the people His protection and provision, and He would fulfill His promise to give them the land of

Canaan—but He would not go with them into the land (see Exodus 33:1–4).

> # We shouldn't settle for God's protection, His provision, or even the Promised Land, without His presence.

Many Christians today don't have the conscious presence of God in their lives. We shouldn't settle for God's protection, His provision, or even the Promised Land, without His presence. When we have the presence of God, we need nothing more—and we should settle for nothing less.

Hindrances to Enjoying God's Presence

I want to share with you two hindrances that will rob us of God's manifested presence in our lives.

Direct Disobedience (Exodus 32:7–8)

Many people confess faith in the Lord Jesus, but do not have His presence in their lives. When we willingly and knowingly disobey God, we grieve the Holy Spirit. When we grieve the Holy Spirit, we quench the Spirit (see 1 Thessalonians 5:19). The Holy Spirit is to us what the pillar of cloud and of fire was to the children of Israel (see Exodus 13:21–22). The Holy Spirit is God's manifested presence in our lives. When we deliberately disobey God, we grieve and quench the Spirit, and when we do that, God ceases to be real in our lives.

Divided Devotion (Exodus 32:4)

An idol can be in the form of anything that you might place in a higher priority over God. It's anything we love more, fear more, serve more, and trust more than God. Is there anyone or anything in your life that has preeminence over Him? Is there anyone or anything that is a greater controlling factor of our behavior than God? Is there a relationship that means more to us? Is there a treasure that means more to us? Is there anything that gets more of our attention than God?

Moses did not want to go without the Lord's presence. We must not settle for anything less.

Experiencing the Presence of God

The presence of God finds its greatest expression in Immanuel, God with us. God Himself comes to save. Jesus Christ, the Son of God, entered human history to give His life as a ransom for many. In His grace, God bought us back in the most unimaginable way possible: in Christ, God became a man, walked among humanity, and died for His people.

In this merciful act, Christ reconciled us to Himself and reopened access to the Father so that those who were once exiled from His presence might again draw near to

God. The purposes of the church are tied to the presence of God. The New Testament calls the church a temple for a reason.

The gospel life—is about being in God's presence. This is why David proclaims, "In your presence there is fullness of joy; at your right hand are pleasures forevermore" (Psalm 16:11 ESV). When we push all our issues away, this is all that is left and all that really matters.

When it feels as though God is far away, here are a few ways I have learned that you can experience and sense His presence.

1. Be Honest with God

Sometimes you can't sense God's presence because there is something blocking the communication between the two of you. He hasn't left, but your sensitivity to His presence might be affected by unconfessed sin in your life. David the psalmist said,

> When I kept silent [about his sin] my bones wasted away through my groaning all day long. For day and night, your hand was heavy upon me; my strength was sapped as in the heat of summer. Then I acknowledged my sin to you and did not cover up my iniquity. I said, "I will confess my transgressions to the Lord." And you forgave the guilt of my sin. (Psalm 32:3–5)

If you feel like God isn't around because you haven't spent quality time with Him, or because you have avoided the thought of Him for so long, confess to God what is on your heart and mind and ask Him to give you an ear to hear His voice again. 1 John 1:9 tells us, "If we confess our sins, He is faithful and just and will forgive us our sins and purify us from all unrighteousness."

Friend, the evidence of God's presence is within and all around us. One common barrier to experiencing it is our tendency to get lost in our own imaginations. This is the barrier, the door, between us and God. We need to die to the worried, preoccupied false self and learn to see with new eyes. Jesus spoke of this death and rebirth when he said, "Very truly I tell you, unless a kernel of wheat falls to the ground and dies, it remains only a single seed. But if it dies, it produces many seeds" (John 12:24).

Removing the barrier of ourselves, distractions, and our motives involves spiritual discipline of prayer and true humility to acknowledge our faults and to seek God's mercy and forgiveness. It involves asking for God's help to remove the falseness that stands between us and the realization of God's presence. When your fellowship with Him is restored, the communication can flow again. So get clean (through the forgiveness of Christ), and let it flow!

2. Speak the Word

When you audibly speak God's inspired Word, you will sense its power and His presence. The Bible says

God's Word is "alive and active [and] sharper than any double-edged sword" (Hebrews 4:12). It's alive! That sharp sword will pierce your heart with conviction & inspiration.

3. Sing God a Love Song

God inhabits the praises of His people. That's why you feel closer to God when you're in a church service, singing hymns or praise songs.

Because that is where worship tends to take place. When you start praising Him, regardless of where you are, you will sense His presence because you are no longer focused on yourself, but on Him. When we open the door of our hearts to love Him, He will meet us there. God is concerned about us knowing him. For us Christians, our first task is to know Him. And out of that knowing, we will come to love Him, adore Him, proclaim Him, and manifest Him. Relationships are established and maintained through communication.

Some of the things in our life are only going to change with prayer. Prayer is God's design to bring about His will in the earth—and through prayer, He has given us the awesome privilege of partnering with Him.

Staying Plugged into the Power Source

I will never forget listening to a sermon, and the pastor was talking about our cell phones; that no matter how much we can do with our phone, when it is not connected to a power source, it is worthless. We can find out all types of facts on our phone; we can even connect with people on the other side of the world. But if our phone is not plugged into a power source, it is useless. May I submit to you that your life is a lot like your cellphone? If you don't connect to a power source daily, the things you do in life are useless.

The secret to praying is praying in secret.

Some of us only pray when we need something. We don't have a routine or a discipline of prayer. Let me ask you this: How often do you charge your phone? All the time! You can't make it through the day connecting with everyone else if you have not plugged into the source. When I was watching that pastor preach, I felt like he was speaking directly to me. He said that as believers, we often set a time for things that take from us, and we don't set aside time for the one who died for us.

In a twenty-four-hour day, can God have just twenty-four minutes? If you want to develop an appetite to spend time with God, you need to know the secrets to a devotional life. We have to get interested in who God is, and then in what He does.

God isn't concerned with our comfort; He's concerned with our character development. Character that reflects Jesus only comes by spending time with Jesus. Until you are with Him, you cannot say that you know Him. The

138

secret to praying is praying in secret. Set a time and place to meet with God—and never miss that time. The key to nurturing your life relationship with God is making it a priority to time to spend with Him. We need to plan our time with Him, and then beat procrastination. Time in prayer is not wasted; time in prayer is invested.

Time in prayer is not wasted; time in prayer is invested.

We get thirsty every day because our body needs water. But our spirit needs God. What would you look like if you hadn't put any food in your body for seven days? You would be malnourished if you lived your life like that! Sadly, many Christians' physical bodies are in better condition than their spirits because they don't communicate with God. They only pray ten-cent prayers and expect million-dollar answers. We need to nurture our daily devotion with Him.

Somebody said, "Your devotion won't start off as a devotion; devotion starts off as a discipline." I have a love/hate relationship with working out, but when I make plans to go to the gym, I'm there—I'm doing it. But after a while of doing the discipline, the discipline turns into a desire, especially when you start to see the results. Now when I miss a day, I'm saying, "Man, I didn't work out today. I need to go work out today." Let discipline turn into a desire!

We pray because it invites God into our life. Prayer is your weapon! Prayer is the thing that goes into situations and changes things when we cannot change them. I have learned that the things we pray for seem impossible, but prayer is the only way impossible things become possible. So many people worry about things in their lives, but if only we would focus on giving Him our worries, and seeking His kingdom, He would take care of the solution. Worry is a conversation you have with yourself about things you cannot change; prayer is a conversation you have with God about things He can change. Worry looks around, regret looks back, but faith looks forward! So many believers need to take out their weapon—it's been put down for too long! Many have been living life powerless, but it is time to connect to the source of Jesus Christ through prayer.

Worry is a conversation you have with yourself about things you cannot change; prayer is a conversation you have with God about things He can change.

If your cell phone was powered by your prayer life, what percentage would you be at? If you don't pray because you are busy, you will lose confidence in your calling and your priority will be lost. The apostles were devoted to prayer and to the ministry of the Word (see Acts 6:4).

Holiness Precedes Power

In Matthew chapter 17, when Jesus was coming down from a mountain, a man approached Him and knelt before Him. He cried out to Lord to have mercy on his demon-possessed boy. The father of that boy said he brought him to His disciples, but they could not drive out the demon. Later, the disciples came to Jesus and asked Him why they couldn't drive the demon out. Jesus's response was because they had little faith, and He explained that the particular spirit they had encountered would only come out by prayer and fasting.

We cannot expect to do what Jesus did without doing what He did. So many want to have Jesus' public ministry of power and authority, without first duplicating His private ministry of prayer and devotion. Prayer is our passport to spiritual power. There is power in persistent prayer. If we replace prayer and the Word with other busy things, we will become casual. Casual believers don't produce power. Every time a believer develops a close, personal, continual, progressive relationship with God in private, they can then carry His power in public. Ephesians 3:20 says God "is able to do immeasurably more than all we ask or imagine, according to his power that is at work within us."

I read a book by Apostle Guillermo Maldonado about fasting where he explained that such active, working power within us comes by virtue of relationship. The power works when we constantly spend time with God. When was the last time you spent time in God's presence and received fresh power? Apostle Guillermo stated something that I will never forget. He explained how when we pray and fast, God will deposit His power in us. This man of God said that the more of God's presence we carry, the faster the power will be activated and released; the more we pray, the more quickly miracles will manifest. We see this pattern in Jesus's life. He continually spent time in the presence of God, and when He went out to minister, the power fell.

Praying is *not* a spiritual gift; it is an invitation to partner with God for kingdom advancement. Angels hearken to the voice of His Word when the words of your mouth align with His will. So many want to live holy lives like God commands, but they don't want to pray. If you don't pray, you will be separated from holiness. Friend, life without prayer has words, but no power. If we don't pray, we will lose our sensitivity and awareness of His presence. It brings a sense of distance that makes you hide yourself from God.

When you stop praying, your spirit moves away from worship and begins to deviate from all holy acts. If we do not pray, we will depend more on things other than God. Prayer is the password to your miracle.

I believe the church needs a conversion to its forgotten first love: Jesus. The closer you come to Him, the further you go from your sinful ways. A sinning person will stop praying, and a praying person will stop sinning. You will either allow prayer to drive out the sin in your life, or you will let sin drive out prayer from your life. God longs for fellowship with you. To Him, every minute is precious. The more minutes we give Him, the more secure we are with our ministry, with our life, and with tomorrow.

How Many Minutes Will You Give God?

A man of God told me something else that I will never forget. He said that longevity in ministry depends on how many minutes we give Him privately. Every minute extends our longevity. Think about time with Him being the root of a tree or the foundation of a building. How deep the foundation is determines how high it can go. The deeper you go with Him in fellowship, the higher you can build, and then the more your ministry will remain and the more your walk will remain.

Let go of everything you think is important that is not. It is time now for us to say no to the things that hold us back from spending quality time with the Lover of our soul. We have to make appointments with God. Your time with the Lord must come first before anything else. Matthew 6:33 says, "But seek first his kingdom and his righteousness, and all these things will be given to you as well."

Why do we pray as Christians? We pray because it builds our relationship with Jesus; it is what helps us overcome temptation and determine God's will. Prayer accomplishes God's work, and it is a weapon of spiritual warfare, a prerequisite to spiritual awakening; prayer is valuable to God! We struggle so much with prayer because of the thoughts that pop in our minds, and all of the distractions that suddenly pop up when we're trying to pray. We need to learn how to take every thought captive and die to our flesh. We cannot control the thoughts we have, but we can control the thoughts we keep. In my spiritual life, I've discovered that every day is an opportunity to either strengthen your relationship with God or neglect it. Your rate of growth is determined by what you feed your spirit. We need to make the word a priority in our lives, because what strengthens your spirit weakens your flesh.

We need to also mix prayer with the word. The devil's weapon is lies; our defense is the Word. God's Word is what generates life, creates faith, produces change, frightens the devil, causes miracles, heals hurts, builds character, transforms circumstances, imparts joy, gives strength, overcomes adversity, defeats temptation, infuses hope, releases power, cleanses the mind, renews the soul, gives life to the spirit, and guarantees our future forever! It is spiritual nourishment, and we must have it to fulfill our purpose. But in order for it to accomplish its purpose and to transform our lives, we must be willing to accept its authority in our lives—and this is the difference between a churchgoer and a disciple comes into play.

If you desire to become a disciple of Jesus Christ, the Bible must become your priority. Perhaps you are not aware, but you have been enlisted in the army of the

Lord. I would suggest you respond to God's invitation in the secret place—and report for duty every day with your armor on and your weapons locked and loaded. Your life may depend on it. Your brothers and sisters need you. Your nation and the world around you need your prayers!

If you desire to become a disciple of Jesus Christ, the Bible must become your priority.

Who knows—perhaps God is waiting for you to become a team player before He promotes you into the next season of your ministry. The invitation is yours. The responsibility is yours. Not only does prayer draw you closer to the Lord, but your prayers also form a measure of covering for others. Don't neglect your part in protecting your brothers and sisters from the schemes of the enemy. This is real war, and lives are at stake. Eternal destinies are at stake. Will you rise up to the challenge to crucify your flesh, engage your spirit, and pray? Will you nurture a lifestyle of daily devotion with Christ? Will you respond to God's invitation?

CHAPTER 10: MORE THAN A HEARER

CHAPTER 10: MORE THAN A HEARER

Some of us are discouraged in our walk with God because we have refused to be doers of the Word and not just hearers. I've learned in my spiritual walk that boldness and courage is what we need in order to be doers of the Word. We need to overdose on courage and let the Holy Spirit mark us with boldness! Nothing in life or in ministry ever happens apart from courage.

I want to take you through Joshua chapter 1, where God comes to Joshua personally to give him a description on courage. At this point, Moses had died before the Israelites could come into the Promised Land because he had disobeyed God. He allowed the pressure of those following him to get to him and he acted in unbelief. So he commissioned Joshua to carry on.

Like Joshua, we need to have courage, because courage enables us to be doers of the Word. I want to share four keys about courage that are found in Joshua chapter 1.

1. Courage Comes When God Empowers

There is no such thing as courage apart from mission, just like there is no such thing as faith apart from challenge. You're not just courageous to be courageous, but you are courageous *for* a purpose.

Moses, a man of God, had died, but nothing of God died. Joshua was chosen. God reiterated to Joshua what he had told Moses to do. I heard someone say, "God doesn't need worthy men—He makes men worthy."

God knows what He's doing. Ephesians 2:10 implies that we should step out in bold obedience. We should walk in the good works He has prepared beforehand. What are the things God has prepared for you to do? What are the things that God has given you a passion for? I've learned that your courage will rise when you have confidence in the call. Most people leave the ministry because of confusion and a lack of courage, but I am here to let you know that God wants to give you fresh courage, fresh fire, and fresh passion.

For someone to act, something is required by the person who is receiving input. We have been filled up to be poured out! Secular people have heard nothing but negative things about the church. It is time for the secular world to see how true Christians act. We have a powerful opportunity to spread our love to our communities, to invite the lost in, and to embrace them and show them the love of Christ!

2. Courage Flows from His Presence

His presence is everything! I've learned that when you host the presence of God in private, you carry the power of God in public. God never calls us to do anything apart from him. Every assignment that God gives, His grace empowers us to carry it out. God's assignments come with a special awareness of God's presence, also known as an unction or anointing.

Do you think God would leave Joshua by himself? If God has called you, then He is with you. Courage does not mean that you are not afraid. It means that you fear God more than you fear your environment. It means that you trust in Him more than anything else.

When you host the presence of God in private, you carry the power of God in public.

3. Courage Rests Upon Those Whose Gaze Is on Jesus

What I find interesting, is that in this passage of scripture, three times God repeats "be strong and courageous." God does not have a speech impediment. When he repeats Himself, He intends to. God is not bound by the way we're "wired." He never discusses with anybody about how they're wired before He calls them to do something. If you are willing, He will use you.

People are waiting for your immediate obedience! Simon Peter illustrates what can happen when we say yes to God.

One day a large crowd pressed around Jesus while He preached. The Lord wanted to use Peter's boat as a floating platform so He could address the multitude, so He asked the future apostle to push the boat out a little from shore. Peter's obedience to His request paved the way for a life-changing blessing (see Luke 5:1–11).

I will never forget hearing a sermon on this story by Dr. Charles Stanley. It totally changed my perspective on obeying God in small matters. The noisy crowd received the first blessing of Peter's obedience; the people could now clearly hear Jesus's words. The Lord said to Peter, "Put out into the deep water and let down your nets for a catch," and Peter had a second opportunity to say yes or no. But this time, Peter may have felt tempted to decline. After all, he was a seasoned fisherman. He had worked the entire night for a catch, but had returned empty-handed. Now this young teacher—a carpenter, by the way, not a fisherman—was asking him to go fishing again? Here is how he responded: "Master, we've worked hard all night and haven't caught anything. But because you say so, I will let down the nets" (Luke 5:5).

Notice what happened as a result of Peter's obedience—Jesus demonstrated His power and sovereignty. Peter and his friends ended the day in complete amazement because they pulled in not one, but two overflowing boatloads of fish!

Saying yes to the Lord's request resulted in a miracle that transformed not only one fisherman's life, but the lives of the entire group. Obedience is critical to an effective Christian life. Charles Stanley once said, "obeying God in small matters is an essential step for receiving God's greatest blessings."

If Peter had said anything other than yes, he would have missed the greatest fishing experience of his life. But because of Peter's obedience, the Lord arranged a miracle that he would never forget. I have learned that God's greatest blessings come as a result of our willingness to do something that appears very insignificant.

I have discovered by experience that our obedience always benefits others. I remember a few days before New Year's Day in 2018, my cousin was helping me create a website for my Christian clothing line. I planned to bless him with a few hundred dollars for his effort. I felt the Lord impressed on my heart to give him five hundred dollars. As we were driving, he fell asleep in my car. As I pulled up to the ATM, I felt the Lord say, "Do you not trust Me?" I took out five hundred dollars from the bank and placed it in his hands when he got out of my car. He didn't realize at first what I gave him because he was still half asleep, so he thanked me and walked in his house.

The next day I got a phone call from him, telling me that what I blessed him with was the exact amount he needed to pay a bill. My obedience allowed him to be able to pay what he needed. Two days later, it was New Year's Eve, and before I headed to a family party, a couple from my home church invited me over. I drove over to their place, and we fellowshipped for a bit. Before I left, they said the Lord spoke to them to sow into two ministries that year—and I was one of them. They took out their checkbook and wrote me out a check for one thousand dollars. God doubled what I had sown to my cousin just a few days prior!

Think of how many people were blessed by Peter's obedience. Not only could the crowd see the Lord and hear His lesson, but Jesus Himself also benefited—preaching from the boat enabled Him to sit down in comfort while He spoke. Then, of course, Peter's friends had a very profitable day—they took in two boats so full of fish that both began to sink. More importantly, they had the opportunity to witness the Lord's supernatural provision.

In December of 2020, I was headed to Yakima, Washington, to preach. I had to stop in Seattle in order to hop on another plane to Yakima. When I landed in Seattle that Thursday night, my flight to Yakima got cancelled. I had to stay the night in Seattle, so I got an Uber to the hotel. The man driving me was a Hindu. I started sharing the gospel of Jesus Christ with him during the ride, and after a few minutes of sharing with him my experience with the true love and power of God—and that Jesus is the only One who can satisfy His soul—

he looked back, intrigued, and said to me, "How can I know this man Jesus? When we pulled up to the hotel, he got out of the car and prayed with me on the side of the curb. This man encountered the power of Jesus and confessed Him as the son of God! He said he felt free and never experienced this power in his life. Praise God for the flight cancellation! God planned to touch this man's heart at two in the morning in downtown Seattle. There are many different paths you could take, but only one leads to eternal life. Jesus is not one of many ways to approach God, nor is He the best of several ways; He is the *only* way. Many men wanted to be God, but only one God became man.

> Salvation is found in no one else, for there is no other name under heaven given to mankind by which we must be saved. (Acts 4:12)

I have learned that God's call to obedience always demands our response. God often rewards others as a result of our obedience. For example, when a father obeys the Lord, his entire family reaps the reward of God's blessings. Likewise, a child's obedience will bless his or her parents. When we obey God, we will never be disappointed. I am sure Peter assumed that Jesus's fishing instructions would just be a waste of time. But when he complied with the Lord's simple request, Jesus brought about a miracle that gripped the disciple with amazement. Partial obedience is not obedience. After all, how can we obey God halfway? And delayed obedience is still disobedience.

Peter's boat became the Savior's stage. The outcome of Peter's faith now opened the door for what he would do for the rest of his life. Jesus said to him, "Do not be afraid; from now on you will be catching men" (Luke 5:10 ESV). What an awesome way to live the rest of your life!

People have told me, "Matt, I just don't know whether God wants me to do this. It doesn't make sense." I'm sure going back out to fish in the heat of the morning didn't make sense to Peter. No one went fishing then. It was hot, and the fish went to the bottom of the lake—a place where nets couldn't reach. At night, the fish swim closer to the surface of the water.

You see, your obedience today prepares you for your obedience tomorrow, and tomorrow's obedience prepares you for the next day, and for the years to come. What are you doing today that is right for tomorrow? The fish weren't available the night before, but the next day—in the heat of the morning—they were right where God wanted them to be.

There are no coincidences with God. Nothing "just" happens.

There are no coincidences with God. Nothing "just" happens. I believe in divine appointments. He always has a plan. If you want to walk in step with Him, then you will learn how to be obedient.

It's time to be more than a hearer. You might be scared of what can go wrong, but I tell you, friend, it's time to get excited about what can go right. The same sovereign, omnipotent God who keeps your heart beating and the planets orbiting is more than able to handle the results of your obedience. When He tells you to do something, and you know without a doubt it is His will, then you need to obey solely based on who is doing the talking. When you choose to obey the Lord, He will bless you. This is because obedience always leads to blessing.

Start obeying the Lord, and watch Him work in your life! If you act courageously, you will get more courage. God is with you, but He will only strengthen you when you take the step forward. You are a leader! Leadership is strengthened by acts of obedience. It's a verb, not a position. People say they want God to guide their footsteps, but they are not willing to move their feet! He can't steer a parked car. The wind will only blow when you put up the sail. People want to have certainty before they act, but I've learned that it is the action itself that creates the certainty. It is the courage to move and to change one's thinking and one's circumstances that creates the certainty. This is the confirmation. People don't want to have doubt before they act—but it is the action itself that relieves you from doubt.

It's time to become "doers" of the Word. We need to let the Holy Spirit of God move upon us and within us and give us strength and energy and desire to be ambassadors and witnesses for Christ.

4. Courage Is a Byproduct of Living in the Word of God

Our mission is to know God and to make Him known. Proclaim the Word ("let it not depart from your mouth"). Doing the work of ministry cannot be effective without being built upon the Word. We need to learn how to get in Word until the Word gets in us. The Bible says to meditate on it day and night. I've learned that the reason you can proclaim the Word is because you have it stored up within you. It is the background noise of your life. When trials come, you can just turn up the volume. We need to treasure the Word. So many books inform us, but only one can transform us! Immerse yourself in the book. Love it and walk it out. Do all that is written in it.

CHAPTER 11:
FIREBRAND
GENERATION

CHAPTER 11: FIREBRAND GENERATION

T he word *firebrand* refers to a person who is passionate about a particular cause, typically inciting change and taking radical action. I believe this "firebrand generation" that God is raising up will only care about the spirit of revival consuming the hearts of humanity. They will go into the highways and byways proclaiming the year of God's favor. They will preach and make the gospel clear with power leading to the way to heaven, which is Jesus Christ. They will be a generation committed to ministering the gospel with boldness. The spirit of boldness will be all over this firebrand generation. They will minister the spirit of revival with no reservations, no holding back, and no compromise. They will be real with people. They will minister honesty to the people of this world. They will not be a "seeker sensitive" generation, but one that is full of the Holy Spirit grace and power.

In John 1:29, John said, "Look, the Lamb of God, who takes away the sin of the world!" This generation will not seek to use the name of Jesus to promote themselves and their selfish motives. They will seek to be "nameless and faceless," simply wanting to lift up the name of Jesus Christ and put down their own names. This firebrand generation will want nothing to do with entertaining saints at the expense of enlightening sinners. They don't want to be behind a pulpit that puts people in the pews, but doesn't pull people out of the pit. They will spend less time in the spotlight and more time in the secret place.

> ## This firebrand generation will want nothing to do with entertaining saints at the expense of enlightening sinners.

This firebrand generation that God is raising up will not seek secular acceptance at the expense of spiritual approval. They will not get caught up in counting heads instead of changing hearts! They will be a "bless Jesus" generation instead of a "bless me" generation, as the former generations were. Everything this firebrand generation does will be to lift up the Lamb of God, which is Jesus Christ. They will live with the reality that when the name of Jesus is exalted, He will draw all men to His saving grace. They will not just make noise—they will carry a *sound*!

They are full of courage; they heal the sick, cast out demons, and lead people to Jesus. They aggressively take over neighborhoods, cities, and nations. They are full of purpose. They are committed to obeying the Great Commission. They are excited about soul winning. They go after the lost.

They are full of passion. They love God and love people. They are moved with compassion. They are excited about serving God. They are alive. This is what the firebrand generation looks like! Will you respond to God's invitation? Now is the time to move from being a passive Christian to an active Christian!

REVOLUTIONARY.
RADICAL. REDEEMED.

These words sum up the life of evangelist Matt Cruz.

Revolutionary: Born and raised in a multicultural church on the south side of Chicago to parents who both serve as senior assistant pastors, Matt grew up knowing Jesus, but never realizing the fullness of God's power in his life. After attempting paths in law enforcement and the military, an encounter with the Holy Spirit one night in his basement revolutionized the course of his life.

Radical: Matt began evangelizing on the streets of Chicago and seeing miracles come as a result of his obedience to share his faith at all costs. Using social media, his videos of witnessing and encouragement reached over 200 million views. Doors began to open for Matt to travel and share his radical faith all over the United States by co-founding the RiseUp movement, and he is the founder of Till All Have Heard apparel.

Redeemed: As a young man who told his parents he would never preach, now at twenty-four years old, Matt is walking in his redemption as he provokes others to rise up and demonstrate the power and love of God. A powerful young man, Matt Cruz is poised to bring revival fire to this generation and beyond!

Find out more at www.mattcruzministries.com.